PROFANE WASTE

GREGORY R. MILLER & CO.

New York, New York

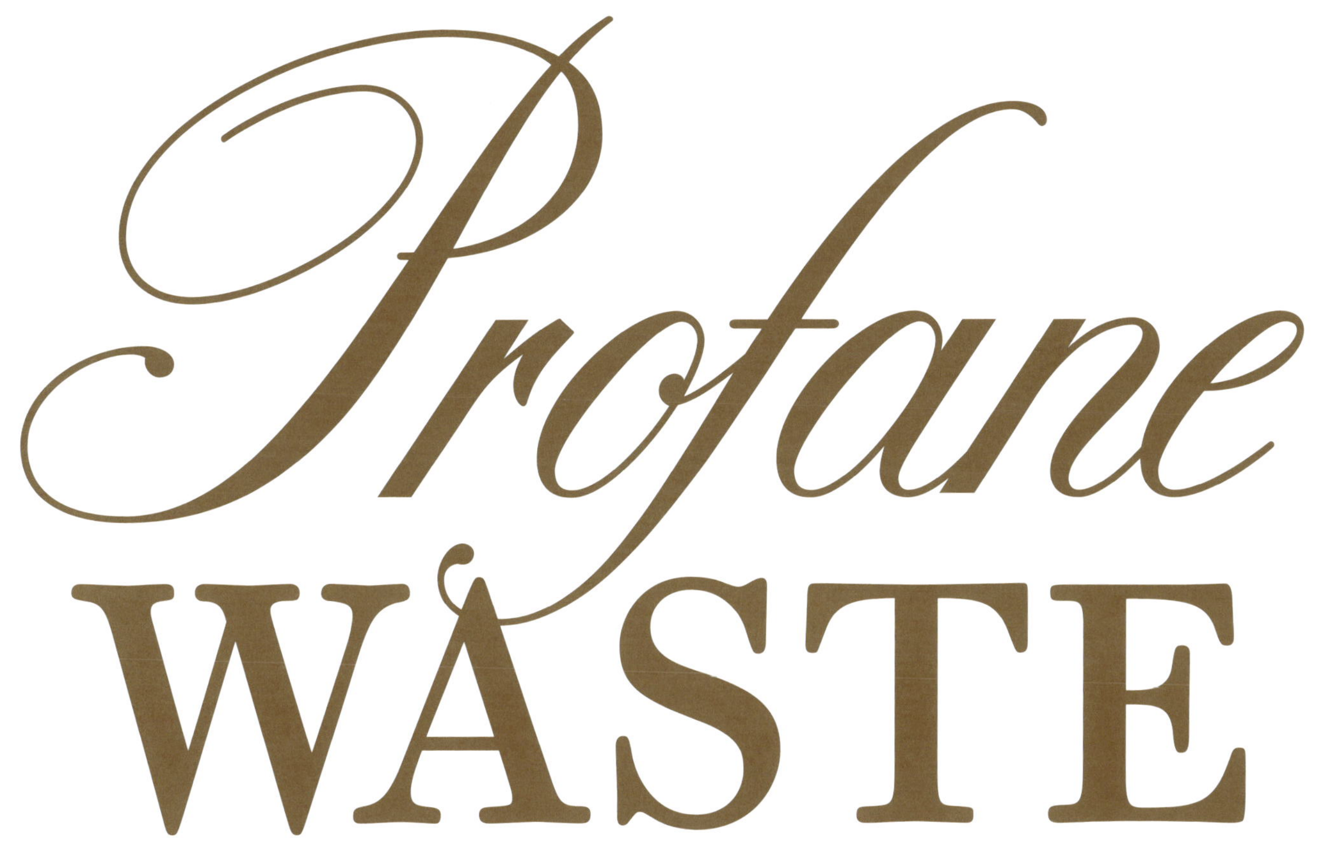

Photographs by DANA HOEY • Essay by GRETCHEN RUBIN

Published in 2006 by Gregory R. Miller & Co., New York

GREGORY R. MILLER & CO., LLC
62 Cooper Square
New York, New York 10003

Book design: Charlotte Strick and Claire Williams
Cover photograph: Dana Hoey

Printed and bound in China

Available through D.A.P. / Distributed Art Publishers
155 Sixth Avenue, 2nd Floor
New York, New York 10013
Tel: (212) 627-1999
Fax: (212) 627-9484

Library of Congress Cataloging-in-Publication Data

Rubin, Gretchen Craft.
Profane Waste / photographs Dana Hoey;
text Gretchen Rubin p. cm.
Includes bibliographical references.
ISBN 0-9743648-3-5 (alk. paper)
1. Waste (Economics) 2. Consumption (Economics) I. Title.
HC79.W3R83 2006
339.4'7<dc22
2005030747

CONTENTS

True Stories IX

Notes on the Collaboration X

I THE TABOO AGAINST WASTE 2

II ORDINARY WASTE AND PROFANE WASTE 14

III WASTE THAT IS NOT PROFANE WASTE 22

IV SPECIES OF PROFANE WASTE: HEEDLESS WASTE 36

V SPECIES OF PROFANE WASTE: DEFIANT WASTE 44

VI SPECIES OF PROFANE WASTE: DENYING WASTE 56

CONCLUSION 61

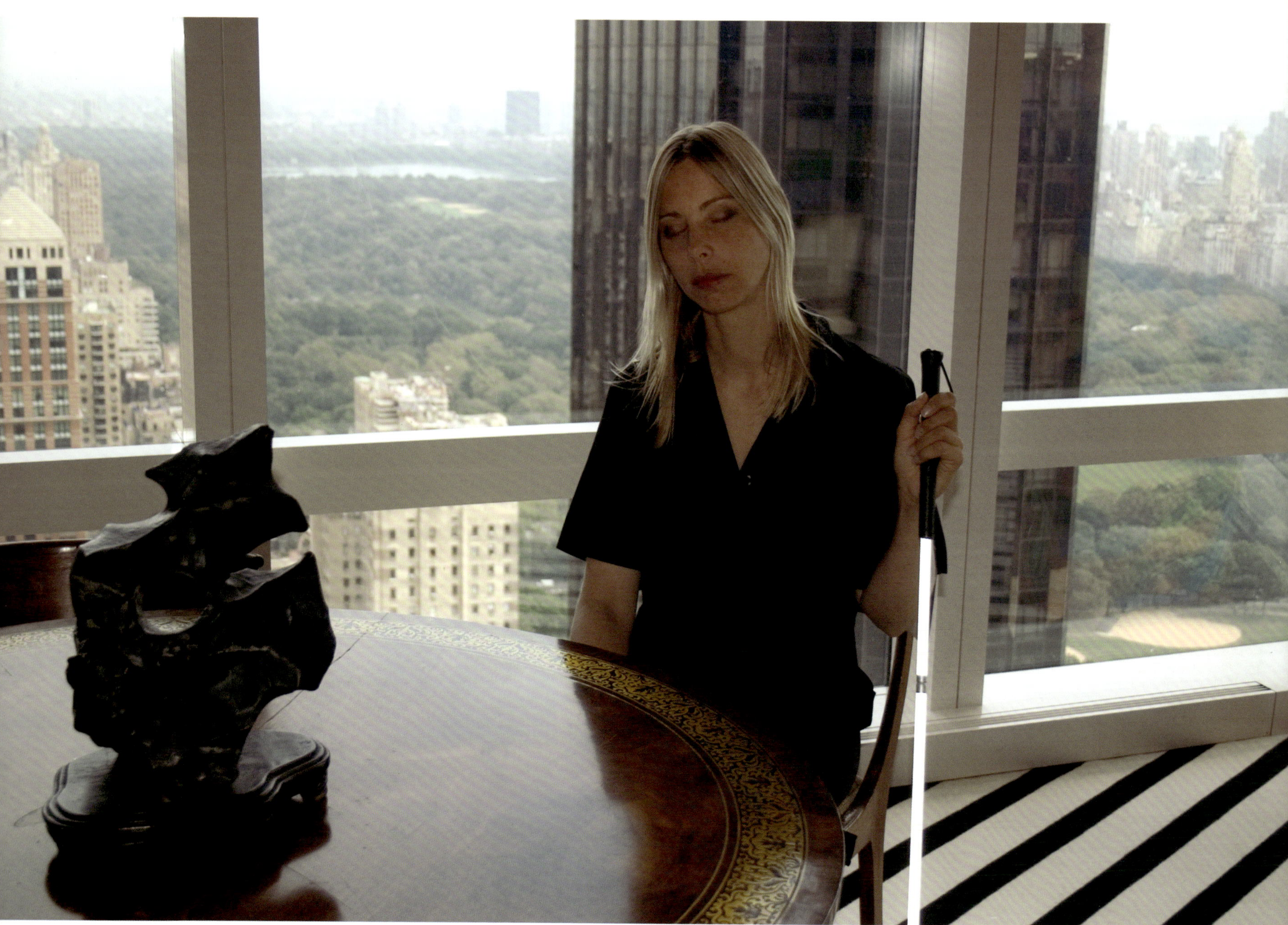

Figure 1 / *The View*

1 *A rich young man went to an art show. He chose a friend's high-priced painting to buy, showily phoned his accountant to arrange a transfer of funds to cover the expense, and handed over his check—then, amid the gallery crowd, he grabbed a wide-tipped black marker and scrawled "SOLD" across the canvas.*

2 *Gertrude Stein quoted Alice B. Toklas: "I like a view but I like to sit with my back turned to it."*

3 *A man stopped by a deli on his way to the office and bought a piece of packaged cheesecake with his cup of coffee. A few hours later, he threw away the cake, still in its plastic wrapper.*

"Why is that in the trash?" asked a friend, pointing to the unopened slice.

"I don't want it," he answered.

"Why don't you keep it for later? It's got enough preservatives to stay good for months."

"No, I don't want it," he repeated. "I just want to throw it away."

NOTES ON THE COLLABORATION

Gretchen Rubin

While in law school, I happened to see a friend throw a newly purchased, never-opened package of cheesecake into the garbage—an action that doesn't sound particularly significant, of course, yet it shocked me profoundly. That single fleeting episode has haunted me for years.

Soon after witnessing that wasteful gesture, I decided to tackle in writing the question of why—contrary to conventional economic expectations—owners might choose to waste their own property and, more interesting, why these actions have such eerie resonance. Why should destruction and loss be so thrilling? My suspicion that I'd stumbled across some unnamed taboo was confirmed when, after I asked a prominent property professor to supervise a paper I wanted to write on the topic, I was told not to bother because "people don't deliberately waste their own possessions." Oh yes, they do.

I did write that law paper, and even went on to write a bad novel that played with the same ideas, but I was dissatisfied with both. Neither the academic nor the fictional framework allowed me to convey the power and mystery of these actions.

Several years later, in New York City, Dana and I crossed paths. We'd known each other since college, but I hadn't seen her for some time. At this point, Dana had become a well-established artist, and I found her photographs tremendously potent and provocative. Energized by visiting her studio—and seeing pieces like *Monies* and *Bikini Brawl*—I hoped we could find some project on which to collaborate. Then, over coffee one morning, after Dana had read my essay on profane waste, we realized that this was a subject that we wanted to grapple with together.

My writings had frustrated me because even when I felt I'd captured my concept of profane waste, mere words couldn't manage to shock, to dazzle the reader in a single moment. The density and immediacy of Dana's photographs, however, could capture the explosiveness of profane waste as words alone could not. Working together, we could present a vivid account of this rich, strange phenomenon. And so we undertook *Profane Waste*.

One thing we discovered during our collaboration was that we embody both sides of the waste taboo. Dana loves profane waste gestures—in her shooting, she was exhilarated by the burning of a hundred-dollar bill (an actual hundred-dollar bill, not a fake) and by the ruin of a thousand-dollar outfit she'd given to a messy young painter to wear in the studio and by the spectacle of me ironing her photograph *Uptown Downtown*. She loves the power that comes from deliberately and violently editing her own images. I, on the other hand, feel the taboo so strongly that I recoil from profane waste gestures, though I'm mesmerized by them—obviously—at the same time.

I'm pleased that Dana used me as a subject in photographs such as *Dewar's Mother* and *Storage*. Playing this role gave me insight into how she works and thinks, and how the notion of profane waste could be revealed in an entirely different way.

In the end, our goal for *Profane Waste* was to force into view a category of action that hasn't been properly recognized and understood. Profane waste gestures may seem irrational, and their uncanny significance inexplicable, but with this project, Dana and I hope to lay bare intentions that stand outside conventional goals of acquisition and accumulation.

Dana Hoey

I met Gretchen through her college roommate, Megan Matson, who is the *Pregnant Smoker*. I remember a foggy moment (my own), pierced by Gretchen's voice, speaking crisply and brilliantly about group dynamics. I immediately wanted to pit people against one another to reveal social dynamics—a practice that has defined my photography.

Later, we spoke about the vagaries of power money fame & sex for her book of the same name. I was included in Gretchen's book as an example of a "power couple"—which, like a name tattooed on the butt, proved to be unlucky for that marriage. On my way out of that life, I read her elegant essay, "Profane Waste." It came at a critical time, offering a way out of a cul de sac I'd arrived at in my work. (I saw group dynamics; they saw group sex; what the hell.)

I made photographs that reacted to the text right away, photos of people literally performing the act of profane waste. For example, although I was quite broke, a friend and I burnt a hundred-dollar bill for the photograph *Profane Waste*. I could have used Photoshop to change George to Benjamin (and saved ninety-nine dollars). But it was a supernatural, slightly demented thrill to actually enact the ritual.

Photographers have insisted that their images are not just realistic "illustrations"—they stand on their own as art. My work has dwelt on the wall, making an argument for itself painting style. But I'd hit a wall regarding the politico-aesthetic power of such art photography. Each time I produced an image of an aggressive female, capable of acting in the world, the image was flattened and reduced to its tissue-thin cultural essence: sexual viability. Therefore, the photograph's status on the wall, and as its own object, needed to be actively called into question. I loved throwing away the "art" photograph by enforcing a "minor" status in relation to text. This was a way to shift the power balance in my work away from pictorial readings, to the photograph as residue of performance. The images will derive their power not from a macho position on the wall but from being attached to the spine of Gretchen's thoughts.

Breaking the taboo against waste was fun and scary. For *Empty Fountain*, my friend Adrienne and I threw fifty dollars into a fountain, which was incredibly stupid and wasteful. There was a smiling man watching us. I fought the urge to pick up at least the quarters but let it go. Later, we checked and all but the pennies were gone. Whoever picked up the change was just too good for the pennies. Dana S. destroying my fancy suit, dumping dollar bills into pig shit—all these actions were cathartic and liberating. The one thing I absolutely could not throw away was a juicy rack of barbecued ribs.

Perhaps it was destructive superstition to have used only women, and often pregnant women, in these photographs, in hopes of giving them power outside their peculiar, often debased images in the world. I trust the voodoo of profane waste.

PROFANE WASTE

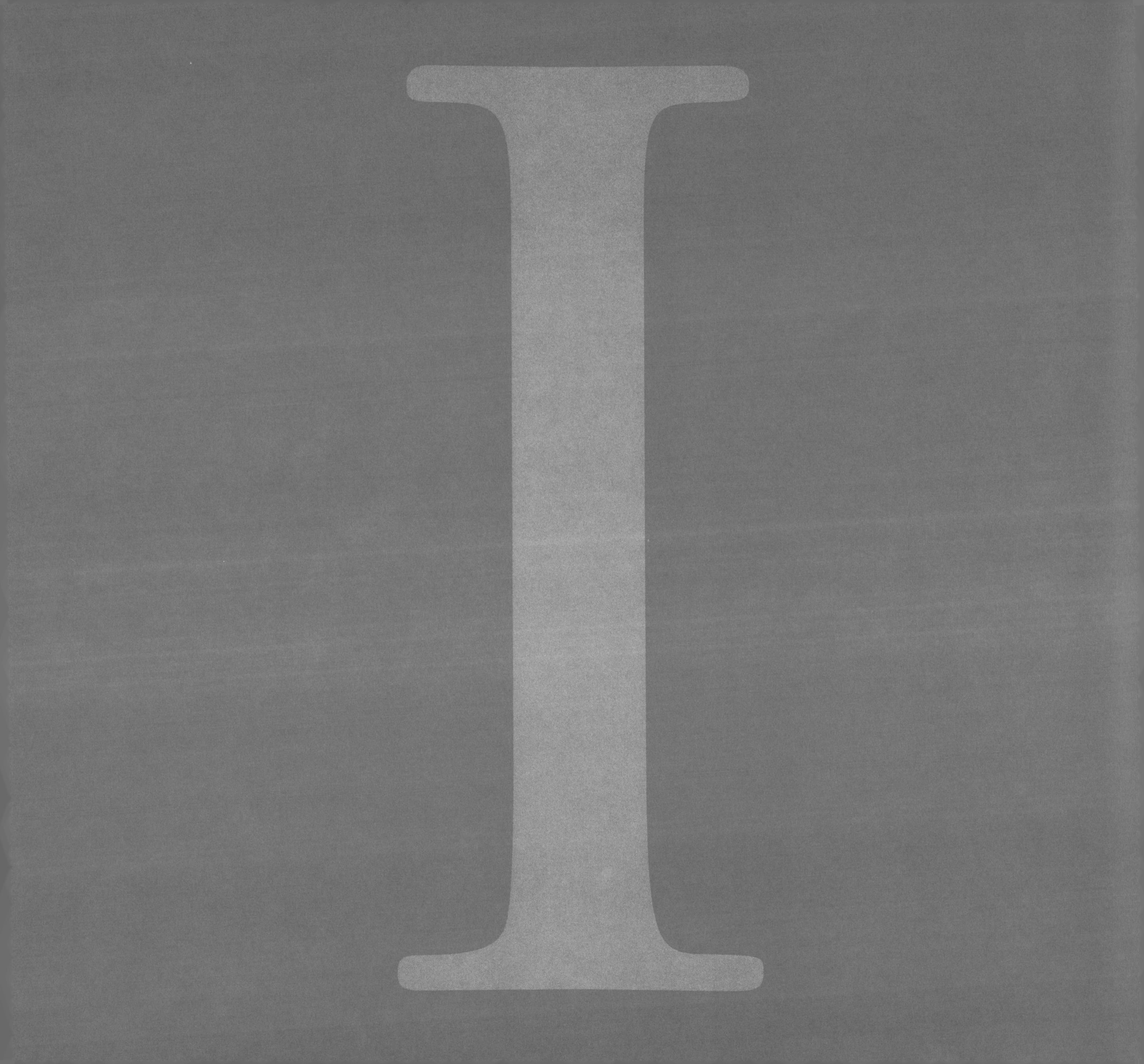

The Taboo Against Waste

....

In our place and time, the popular model of human behavior assumes the goals of economic productivity, acquisition, and accumulation. In other words, men and women are believed to be strongly motivated to become richer, to own more possessions, and to conserve their wealth for their heirs.

This is not to say that such a belief about human nature is true, merely that it is a belief that people actually hold—just as they believe, whatever platitudes they might repeat, that money does buy happiness.

Reflecting this model, most discussions of owners and their possessions focus on property's accumulation and use or, for the more academic, on the philosophical underpinnings of a system of private property.

Traditional classical and neoclassical economists base their theories and models on the idealized behavior of *homo economicus*. This "economic man" is a rational actor who works soberly to achieve gains. Recently, however, behavioral economists have sought to account for striking and widespread economic behaviors inconsistent with reasoned decision-making. For example, prospect theory, which analyzes how people handle uncertainty and risk, describes the phenomenon of *loss aversion*: people act irrationally because they dread loss more than they crave gain. Loss aversion explains unprofitable patterns such as the *endowment effect* (people demand more to give up something they possess than they'd pay to acquire it); the *sunk cost effect* (people tend to continue in a course of behavior, even if unfavorable, if they've made an investment in money, effort, or time); and *status quo bias* (people tend to cling to the status quo because they see the risks of change more clearly than the advantages).

Commentators, however, are much better at explaining loss avoidance than loss seeking. They say little about the *pleasures* of loss, of relinquishment. They do acknowledge circumstances—such as gift giving or altruism—where owners voluntarily surrender their property. But in these cases, owners often expect a return of some kind (a gift in exchange, for instance, or a strengthened social order) and, also, these are examples of voluntary transfers of possessions that continue to exist, not the outright waste or destruction of possessions.

But some owners do choose to waste their own possessions, without return.

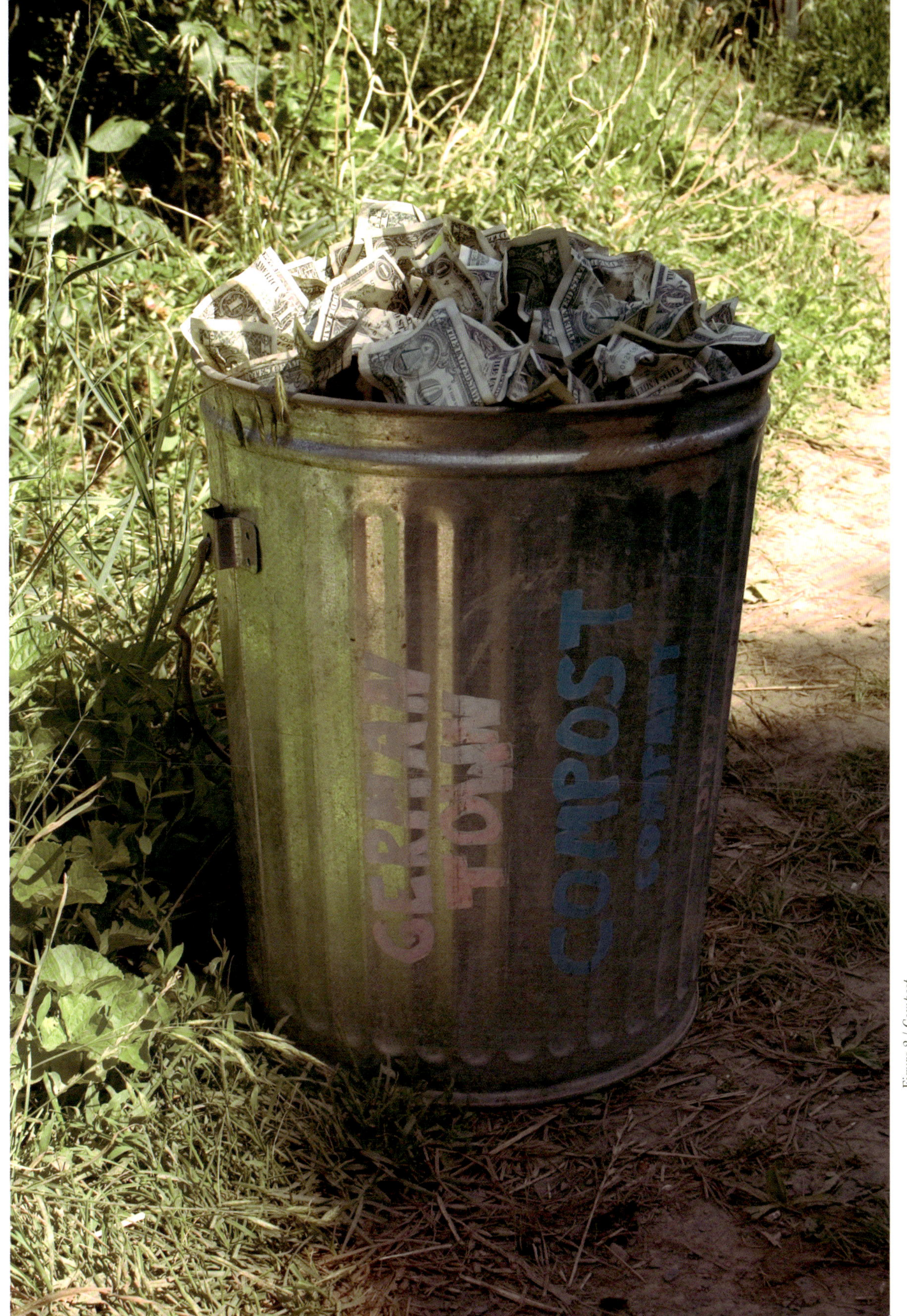

Figure 2 / *Compost*

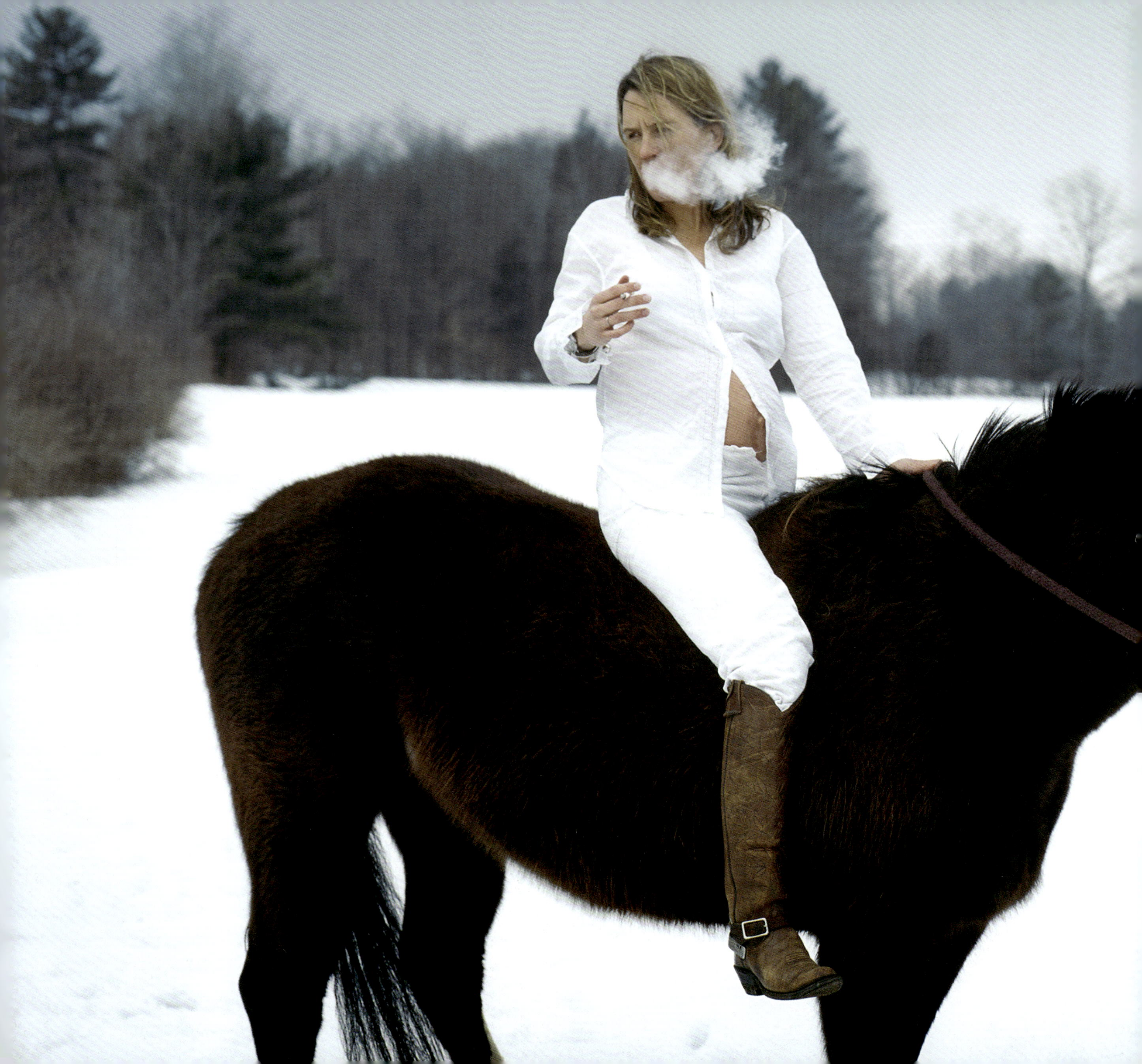

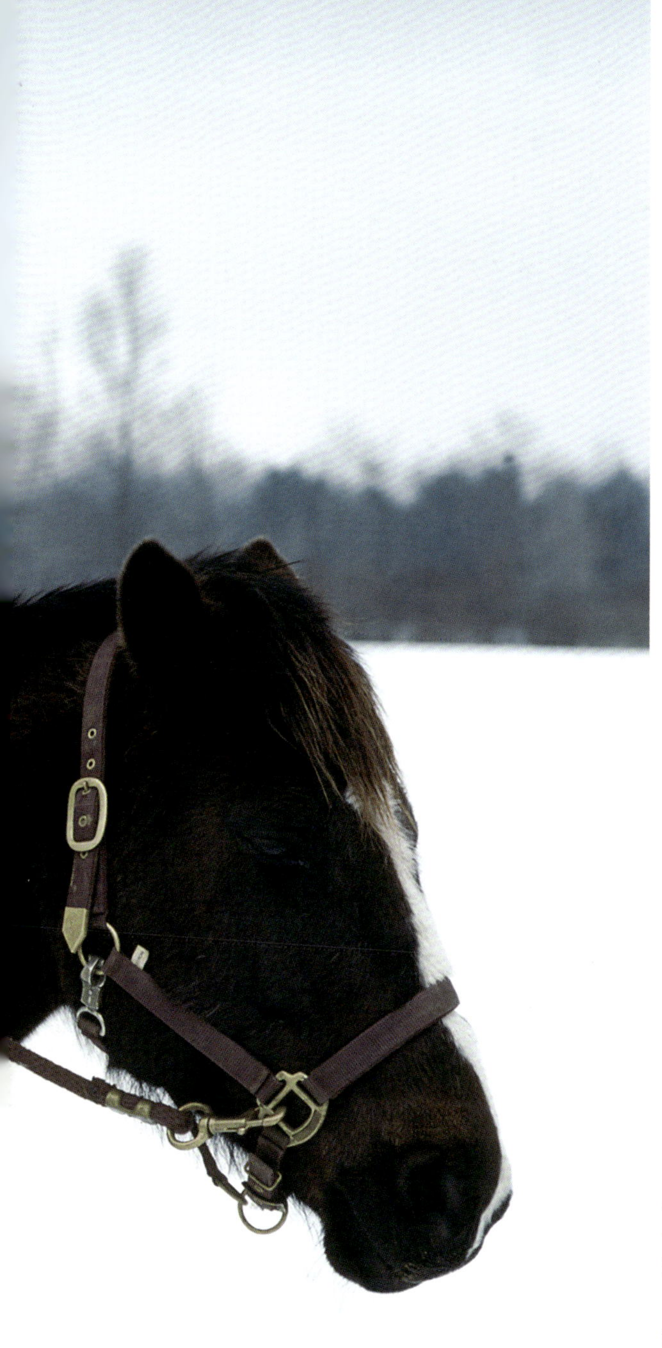

Figure 3 / *Pregnant Smoker 2*

Why?

Why, after toasting his fiancée, would Jack Kennedy urge his friends to hurl crystal glasses into the fireplace? Why would a person delight in walking away from coins that have clattered down a vending machine's change chute?

Such individuals refuse to perform their roles as rational actors making economically prudent choices but instead show a contrary impulse to cast aside or destroy their possessions—and take enormous satisfaction in doing so.

Significantly, whenever an owner indulges such a desire, the action sparks the fascination and disgust of any onlookers. The glee felt by the owner, and the heated reaction of witnesses, signal the presence of an *unnamed taboo*.

A taboo protects what is sacred—a belief so strong as to be beyond question. When a taboo is violated, even those who disapprove—or perhaps especially those who disapprove—cannot hide their fascination.

Conspicuous and familiar taboos constrain sex, blasphemy, drugs, and vulgarity. Rappers and comedians say "motherfucker" and "cocksucker" to invoke excitingly dangerous words. Rebellious teenagers tattoo and pierce their bodies. Robert Mapplethorpe photographed himself dressed in boots and leather, with a bull whip protruding from his anus. Such taboos, however, have been flouted too often and have lost much of their power. But although an erect penis, a defiled Mary, or a dripping needle no longer disturb as they once did, more subtle prohibitions remain.

What's sacred now? Health is sacred. Tolerance is sacred. The Holocaust is sacred. Consider, then, the shock of a seeing a pregnant woman smoking and boozing, of hearing a white professor use the word "nigger" and mean it, of learning that England's Prince Harry wore a swastika armband to a fancy dress party.

What else is sacred? In a market society that draws its strength and energy from exchange, among the most pious observances, people are charged with the obligation—and instilled with a passionate desire—to acquire, to accumulate, if not for themselves, then for their beneficiaries.

After the horrendous events of September 11, 2001, the duty imposed on all patriotic Americans was to go to the mall, to uphold the cycle of producing, buying, and selling. The government exhorted the public to spend a tax refund; the decision to pay down credit card debt or to add to savings was deemed not to be in proper support of the country. This is nothing new. At a press conference in the 1950s, when asked what people should do to fight the recession, President Eisenhower answered:

"Buy."
"Buy what?"
"Anything."

Because national growth and strength depend on continued strong demand, consumers must be persuaded to purchase more. Owners are encouraged to buy, replace, and update; objects are made disposable or touted as "new and improved" to justify owners' abandonment of useful possessions. And in America's culture of insidious and invidious comparison, where the "good life" is defined in large part by possessions, people feel pressed to enlarge and upgrade their belongings to maintain status and even to project identity.

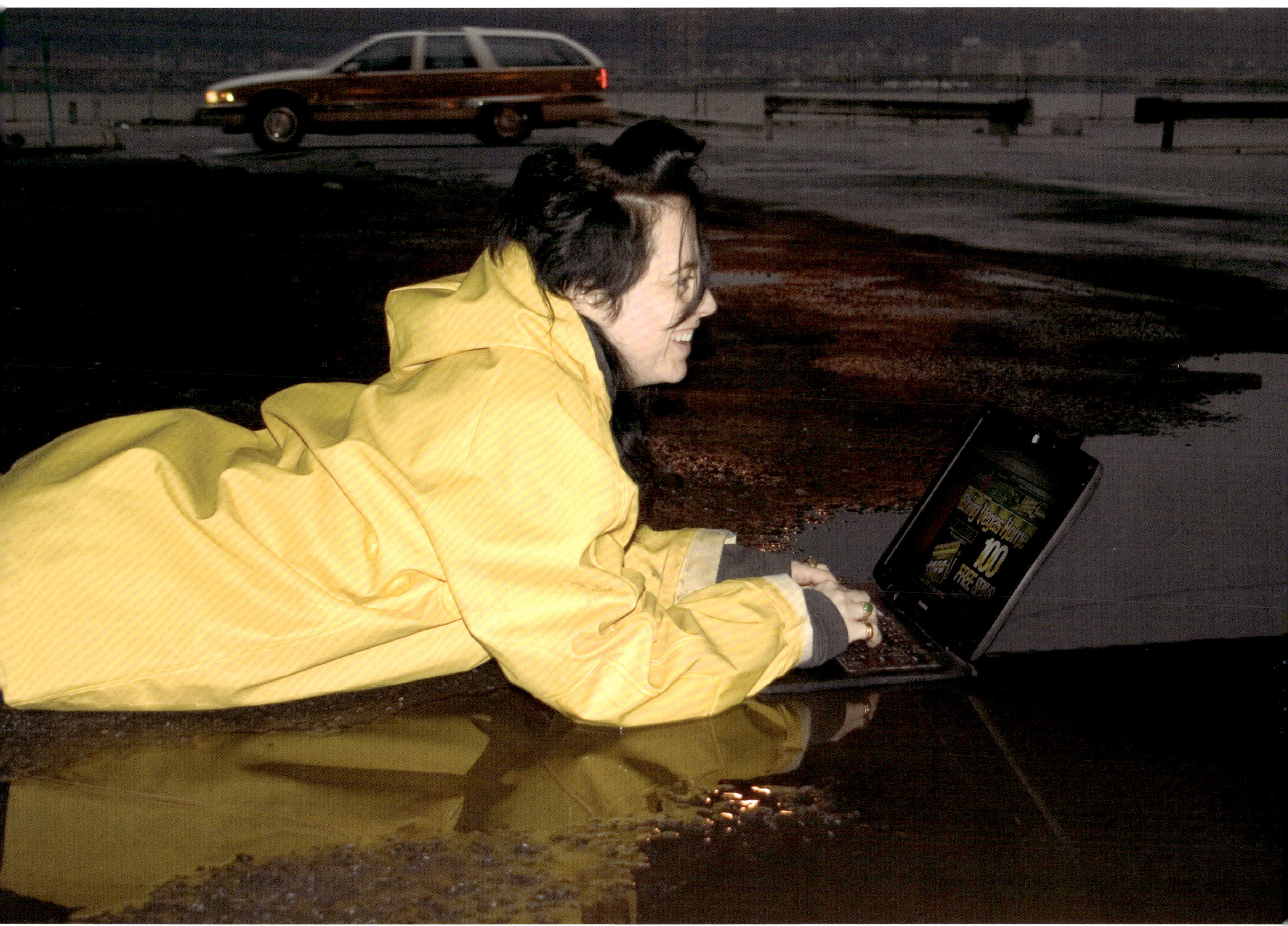

Figure 4 / *Upgrade*

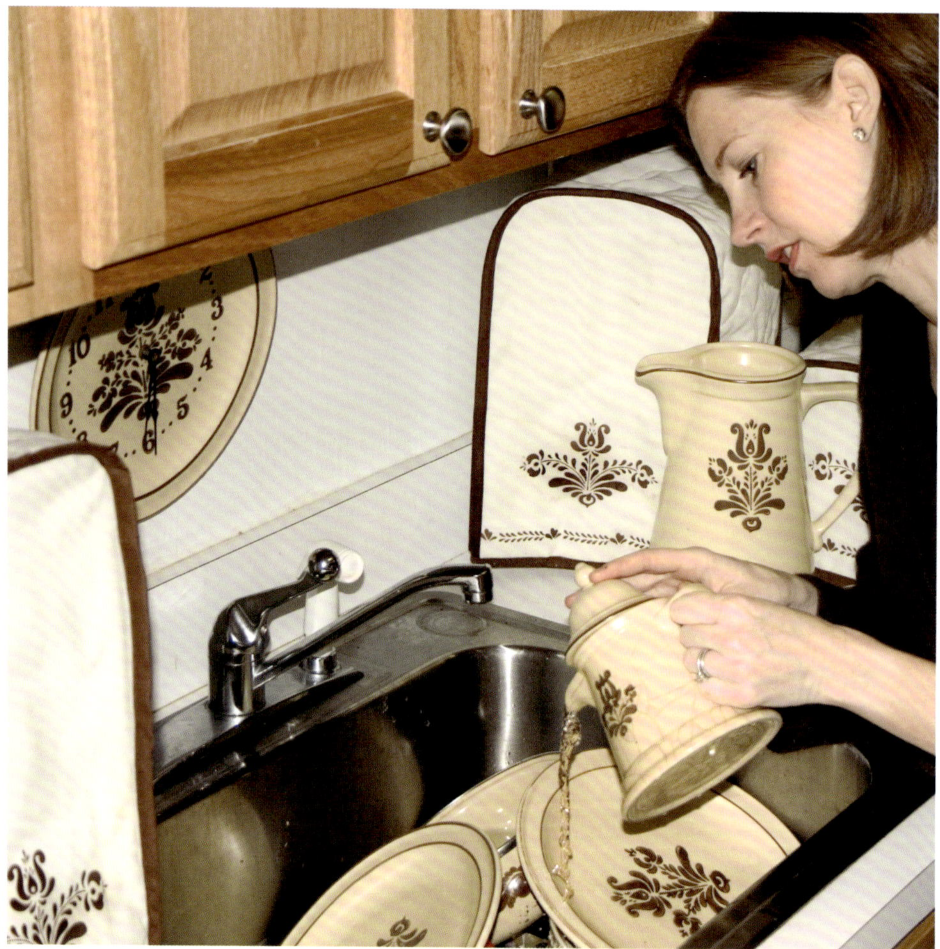

Figure 5 / *Hot Tea*

But although the market economy encourages moderate waste to stimulate trade, it condemns outright dissipation as a violation of the conventional, rational model of property. In a free market that works through voluntary exchange, indulging in willful waste shows a refusal to participate, the desire to take things out of circulation. Also, with our heritage of the Puritans, Poor Richard, and the pioneers, we Americans think of ourselves as frugal, steady, and hard-working—a view undermined by unproductive, profligate gestures.

Our system rests on the principle of balanced accounts, the requirement that income and outflow must square. Its assumptions shape our perceptions, so any significant, deliberate waste violates expected behavior (resource maximization, gain optimization, rational exchange) and is largely overlooked.

One model that does grapple with owners' wasteful behavior is Thorstein Veblen's theory of conspicuous consumption. Wasteful display, Veblen argued, springs from an owner's need to acquire status by visibly dissipating wealth. Veblen's theory, however, doesn't explain all examples of owners' waste of their own possessions, nor does his theory account for the dangerous thrill such action can evoke.

Tellingly, in examples of conspicuous consumption, owners often choose to reverse the waste, if they can do so without losing prestige. At a sixteenth-century banquet in Agostino Chigi's loggia beside the Tiber, Pope Leo X and cardinals ate from silver plates that were grandly tossed into the river after each course; Chigi, however, took the precaution of stretching nets below the water's surface to retrieve the plates after his guests had left. Also, Veblen's theory of *conspicuous* consumption explains only instances of waste that are witnessed; what about the many instances of waste seen by no one but the owner? And why should there be gratification in the very act of waste? There must be some more shadowy desires—deeper even than the desire for recognition and respect—that shape people's wasteful actions.

For, in fact, it is true that on occasion owners purposely and gladly waste their possessions, without any witness or possible rise in prestige. Consider, therefore, this set of disregarded actions, wrongly presumed to be insignificant or irregular, and omitted from most economic discussion: *an owner's deliberate, satisfying waste of possessions, with no expectation of return.*

Call this violation of the taboo against willful dissipation "profane waste."

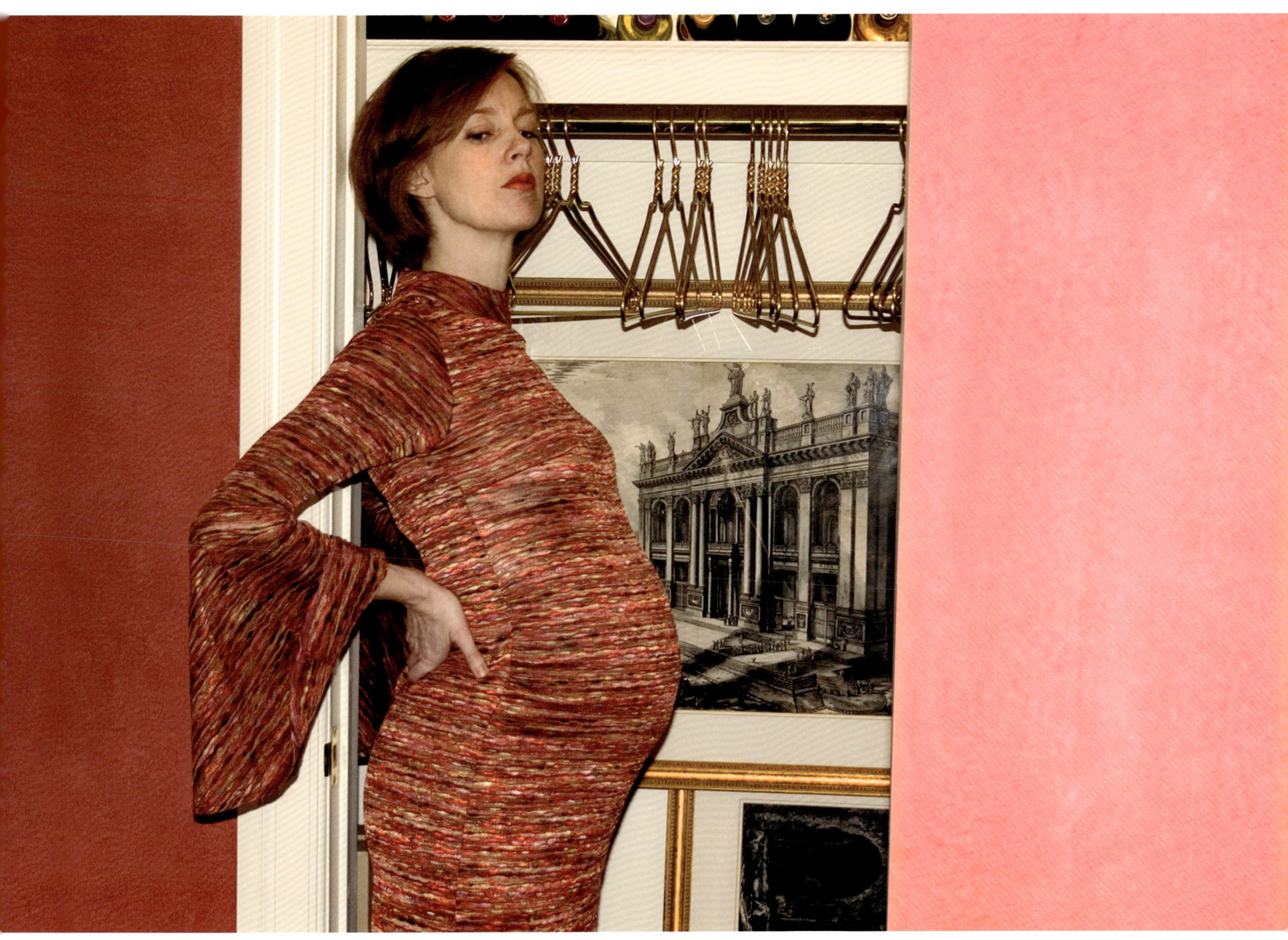

Figure 6 / *Storage*

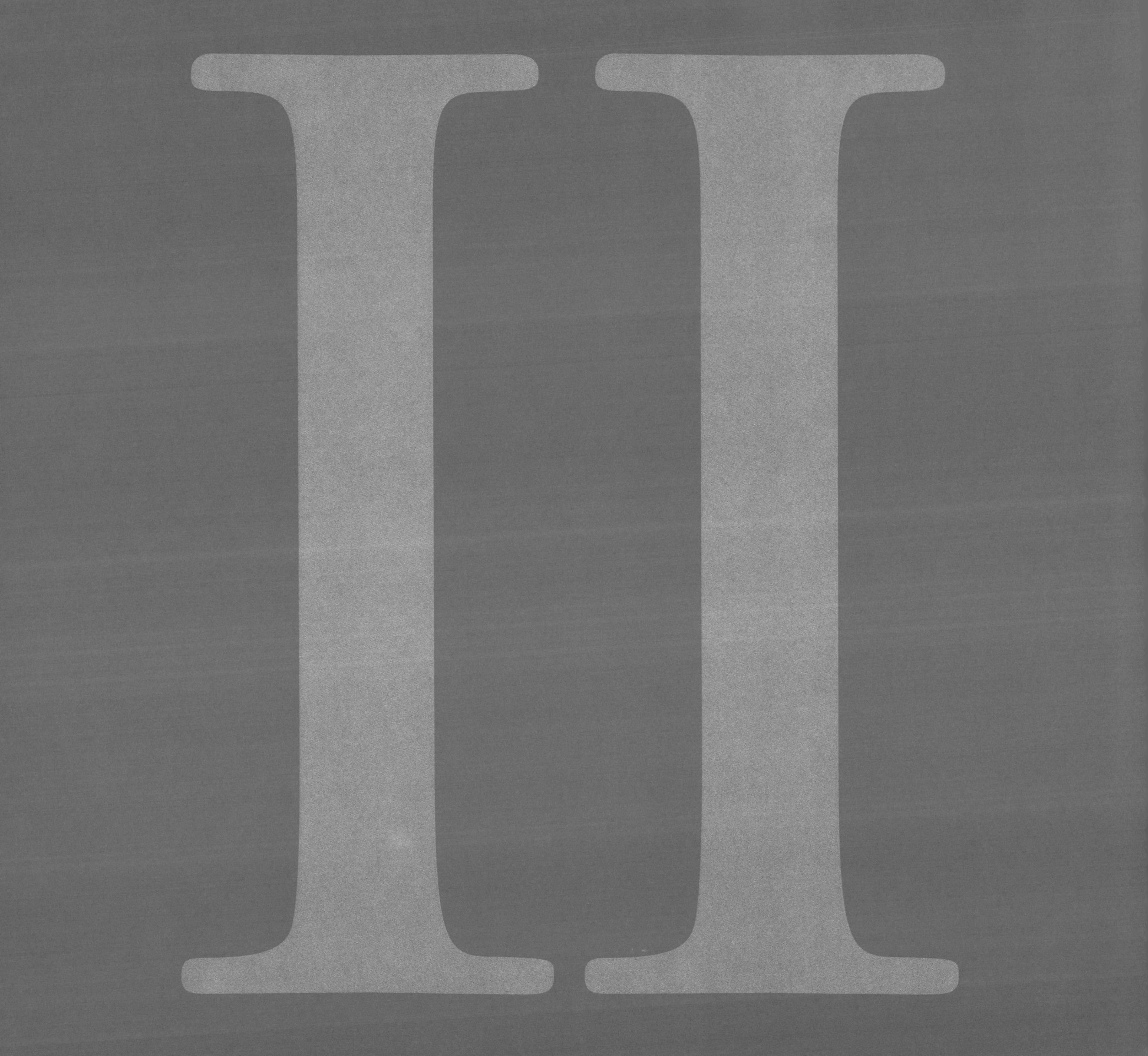

Ordinary Waste and Profane Waste

What is waste? Here, it is the destruction, or the frustration, of the chief purpose of a potentially useful possession or service.

How does profane *waste differ from* ordinary *waste?*

Ordinary waste (practiced by everyone living above subsistence level) produces no thrill and signifies nothing; it's merely the result of custom or laziness or accident. Who hasn't left lights blazing in an empty room?

Ordinary waste provokes regret, frustration, or indifference, while profane waste is exhilarating.

Profane waste requires several elements: first, the waste must strike a person's *own possession*; second, the waste must ignite a *shock of emotion*—of a taboo violated. The waste must be the *source* of the thrill—and the *purpose* of the action—not incidental to the waste. And the owner must have *no expectation of return*. The more valued the thing wasted, the more powerful the reaction in the owner. Profane waste generally involves physical possessions, but it need not.

At its most gratifying, profane waste is expressed through the waste of currency, art, food, gold, or the waste of an object that would ordinarily expect a long life, such as a house or a book or a forest; and where possessions are cast into water, burned, poured out, buried, smashed, or thrown from a height. While witnesses may inflame the excitement of profane waste, it isn't necessary to have an audience other than the owner.

In addition to outright destruction, profane waste can take the form of excessive and redundant spending out. Even for the very poor, some waste is sufficiently modest or conventional to appear routine; to constitute profane waste, consumption must far outstrip the customary level of expenditure. In the White House, Richard Nixon blasted the air conditioner so he could enjoy the perverse pleasure of using a fireplace during the humid summers in Washington, D.C. One person orders fresh flowers for rooms in an unused country house in an act of profane waste, while another buys an expensive brand of coffee beans, then pours away a fresh pot of coffee.

Why do owners violate the taboo that prohibits such behavior? By wasting their own possessions, they flout the relentless demands of necessity. Our dependence on and attachment to the material world are shackles none can escape, but profane waste is an attempt to break free.

Because people are stunned at seeing a taboo violated, and because these wasteful gestures lie outside the popular model of human behavior, acts of profane waste—and the energy released in consequence—are generally misunderstood, even by those who enact them.

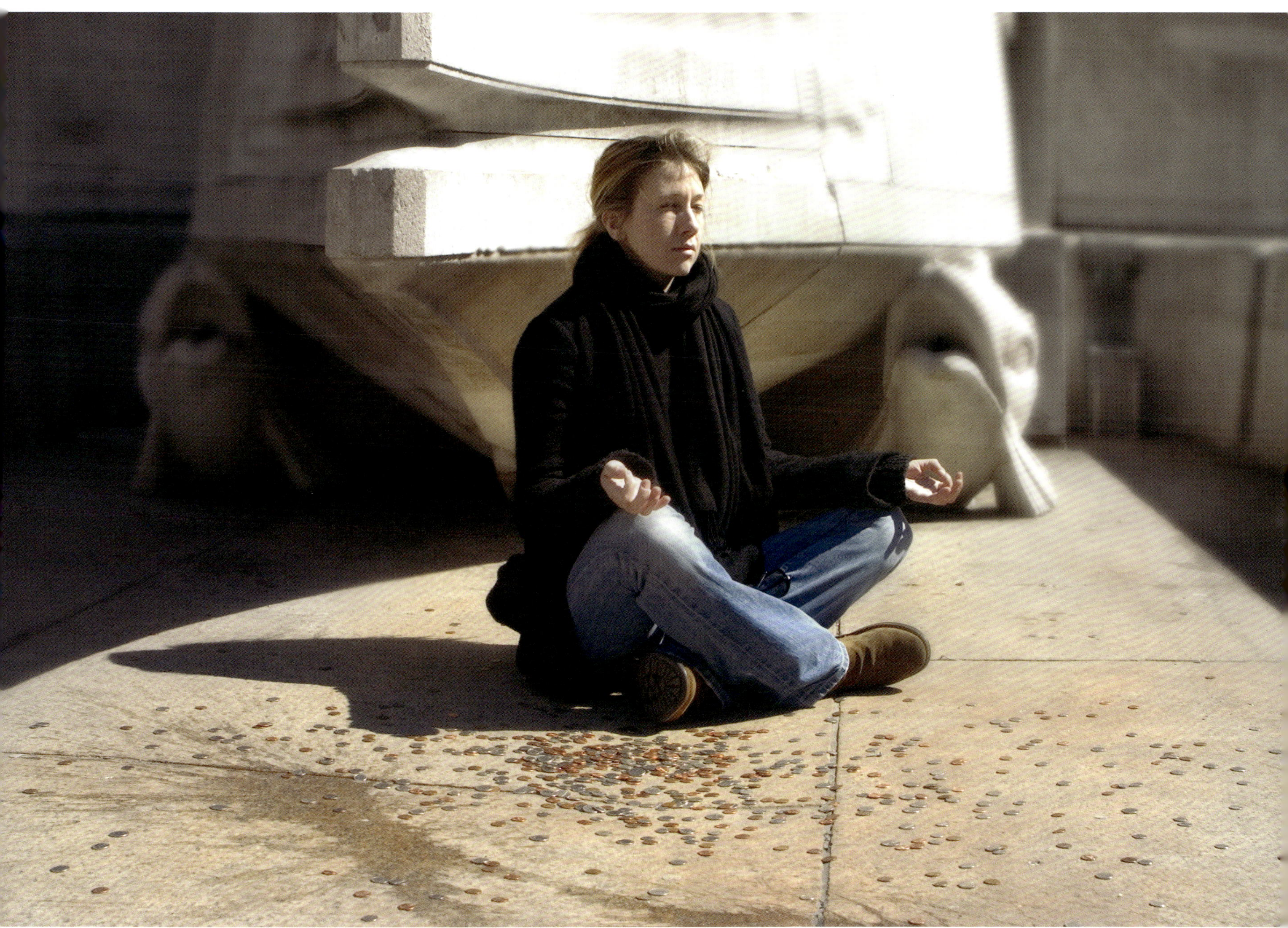

Figure 7 | *Empty Fountain*

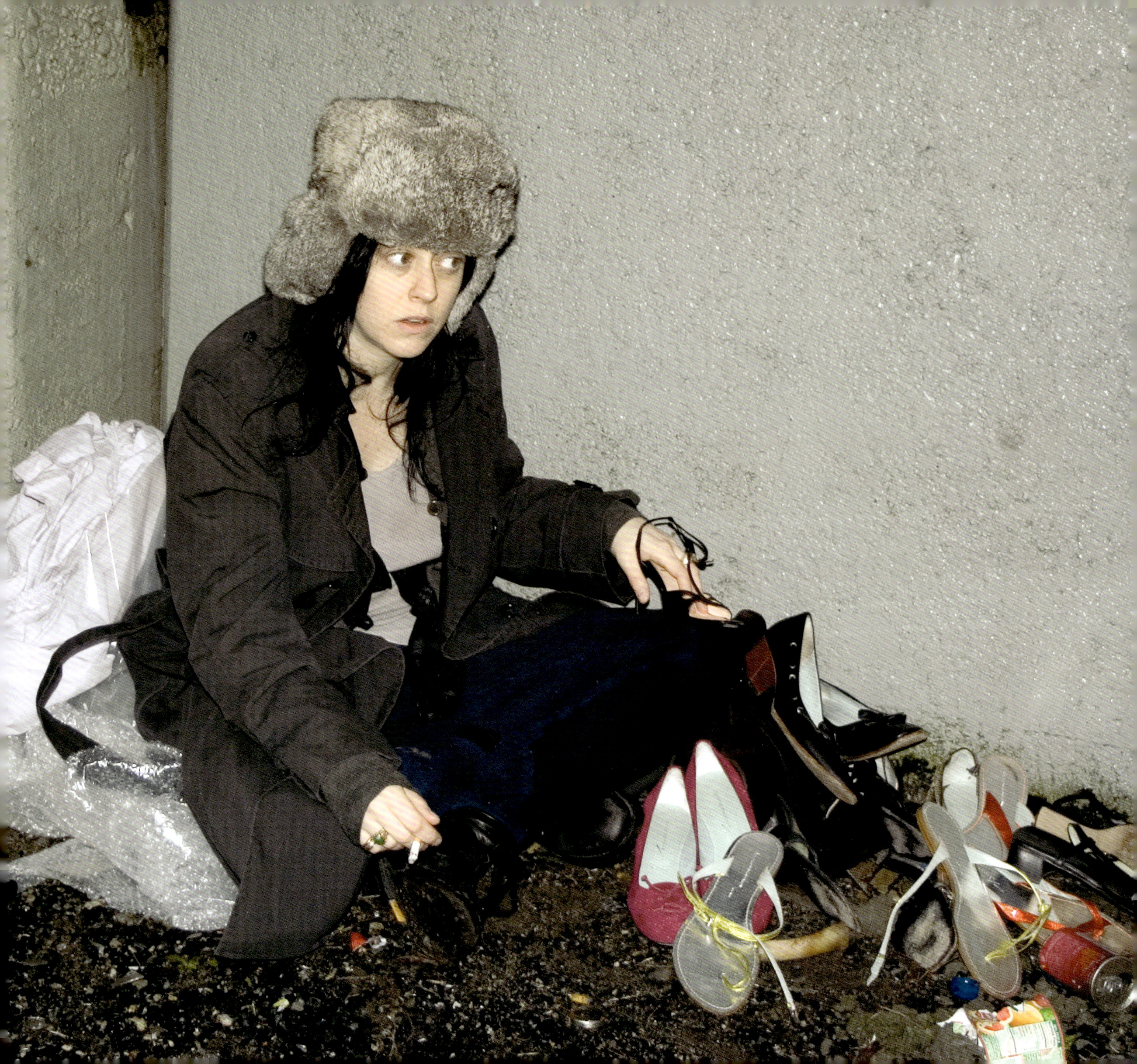

For example, consider Robert Rauschenberg's famous *Erased de Kooning* (1953). Rauschenberg considered this to be a work of art "created by the technique of erasing," but profane waste better explains the work's extraordinary resonance. The actions and remarks of both Rauschenberg and de Kooning reveal that they recognized, if unconsciously, the demands of profane waste; they took care to meet its rigorous requirements.

Rauschenberg wanted to erase a work of art, but he chose not to erase his own work because, he said, he needed a drawing recognized as significant art—it "had to be something by someone who everybody agreed was great, and the most logical person for that was de Kooning." As it happened, Rauschenberg had stolen a drawing from de Kooning, but decided, "That wouldn't do." Why not? Rauschenberg understood that the wasted work had to be his own legitimate possession. After Rauschenberg had erased de Kooning's drawing to nothing but traces of ink and crayon on paper, he placed it in a specially bought gold-leaf frame (*gold* is often present at episodes of profane waste) and kept it in his personal collection for decades.

Figure 8 / *Spent Out* (detail)

No critic of Rauschenberg's work has satisfactorily accounted for the peculiar power of the almost-blank canvas, because it is the force of profane waste that makes the picture explosive. After all, no one would be particularly shocked or intrigued if a collector were to keep the de Kooning drawing locked away in a warehouse forever—even though the drawing would be as invisible to the public as if it had been erased.

Similarly, profane waste accounts for the uncanny appeal of Michael Landy's *Break Down* (2001), in which Landy took all his possessions, from his red Saab to his underwear, and in two weeks, with the help of nine assistants, had these 7,226 objects sorted, labeled, dismantled, and ground into dust by an industrial shredder.

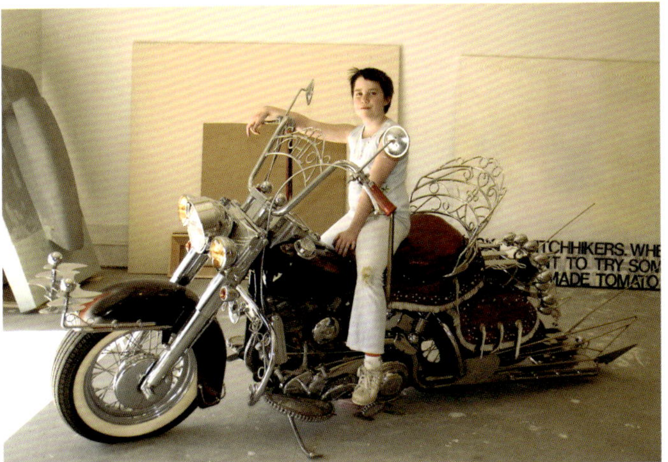

Figure 9 / *Sweet 11*

Break Down met the stringent conditions for profane waste. First, Landy destroyed his own possessions. He made his gesture more profane by including for destruction works by artists Gary Hume, Tracey Emin, and Damien Hirst; the waste of unique and irreplaceable artworks dramatically heightened the shock of his act.

Also, Landy's action flooded him with intense emotions. He described the day after the show opened as the happiest day of his life. "You could say this is a suicide piece," Landy said, "but I don't think it is. I see it as very joyous." And furthermore, Landy noted that although he'd considered making use of his possessions by selling them or giving them away, he decided that the project required that they be destroyed.

Viewers were enthralled by the spectacle; an astounding 45,000 people came to see *Break Down*. Does art appreciation or the thrill of profane waste better account for this tremendous public interest?

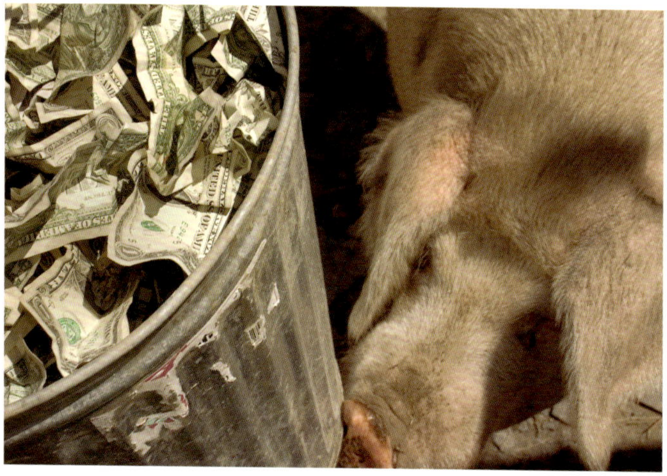

Figure 10 / *Pig Food*

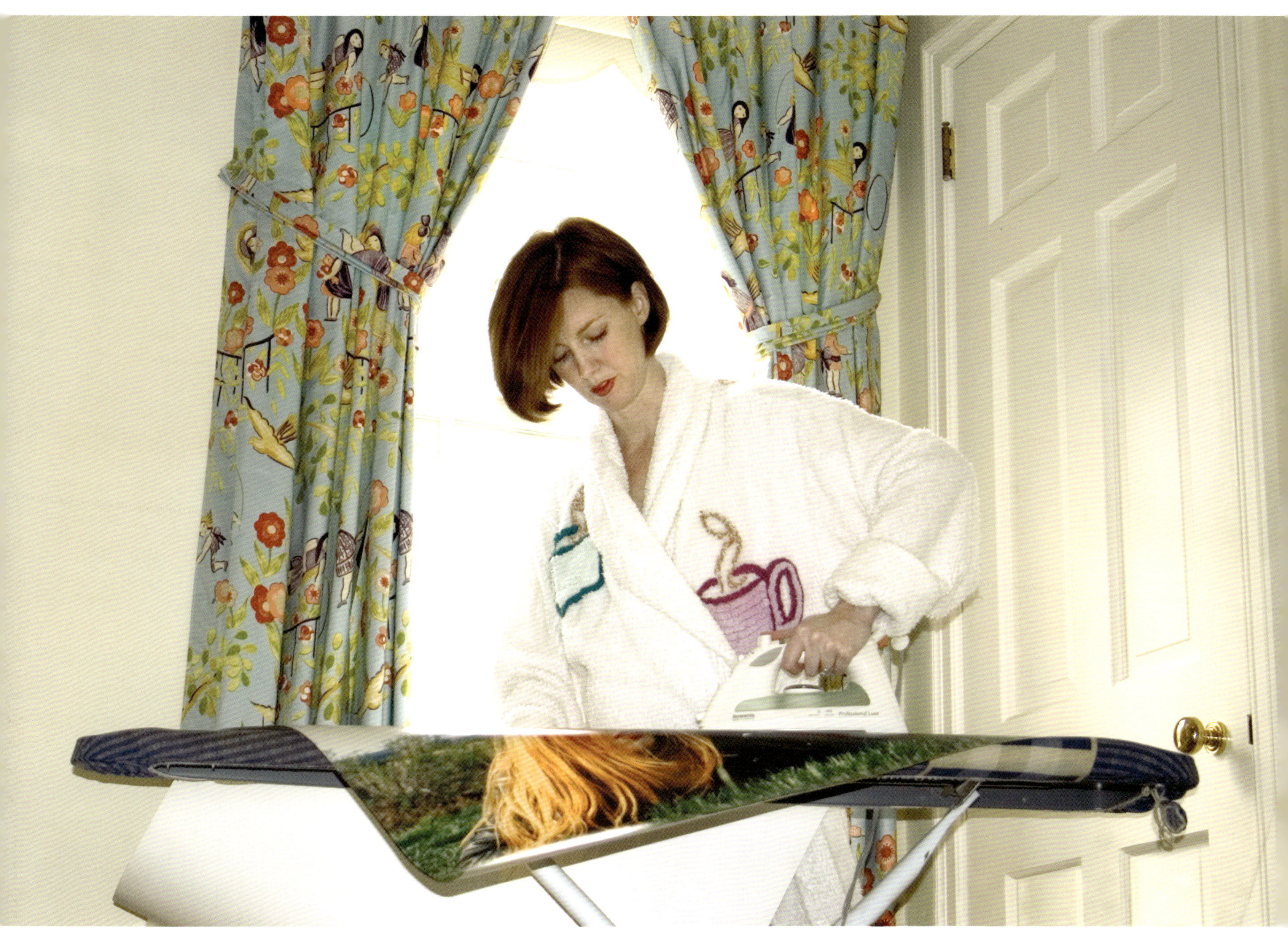

Figure 11 / *Reverse Ready Made*

III

Waste That Is Not Profane Waste

Profane waste takes three aspects: heedless waste, defiant waste, and denying waste.

There are also many species of waste—mostly related to fear or prestige—besides profane waste: gain waste, propitiating waste, hoard waste, host waste, gift waste, status waste, immortalizing waste, witness waste, grab waste, and worthless waste.

Although these sorts of waste can be as compelling as profane waste, they don't satisfy its requirements.

GAIN WASTE, OR SACRED WASTE

To ensure the flow of necessary things, you sacrifice what's most precious (sacrifice is waste compelled by necessity). Although we repeat, "Waste not, want not," gain waste is, in fact, intended to ward off want.

Why does this work?

Gain waste invokes the awesome logic of the principle of balanced accounts: casting things out forces them to return. You accomplish this magical coercion, for example, by dedicating possessions, such as slaughtered animals, to the dead. Now the dead owe you. The ancient Greeks threw wine and bread into the sea to ensure their safe voyage. A person who accidentally spills salt (once rare and precious) must throw salt over his shoulder.

You choose to waste that which you wish to increase: fling coins into a fountain, throw rice at a wedding, cast your bread upon the waters. Artist Salvador Dali tossed fistfuls of bills out of hotel room windows, announcing: "Very important! Everything coming back one million times!" Actress Sarah Bernhardt observed, "It is by spending oneself that one becomes rich." The finer and more costly the sacrifice, the greater the return.

Corporations point to market forces to defend the surging salaries and bonuses paid to their chief executives. After all, why would a company choose to waste its assets by paying more than necessary? But, in fact, the total direct compensation of many top executives has been shown to outstrip what the market would demand as well as to be unjustified by performance. So what explains the exorbitant pay of these CEOs?

These vast sums prove what the corporation can afford, of course, and sometimes they are the fruits of a CEO handpicking a friendly board of directors—but the payments are also a form of gain waste. Rewarding the executives with so much money is meant to ensure that they'll generate fat profits.

In the same way, many hedge fund millionaires pushing their way into the art world welcome the opportunity to spend extravagantly on their purchases. They *prefer* a higher price; paying more seems to force an artwork to become valuable—and so, too, its owner.

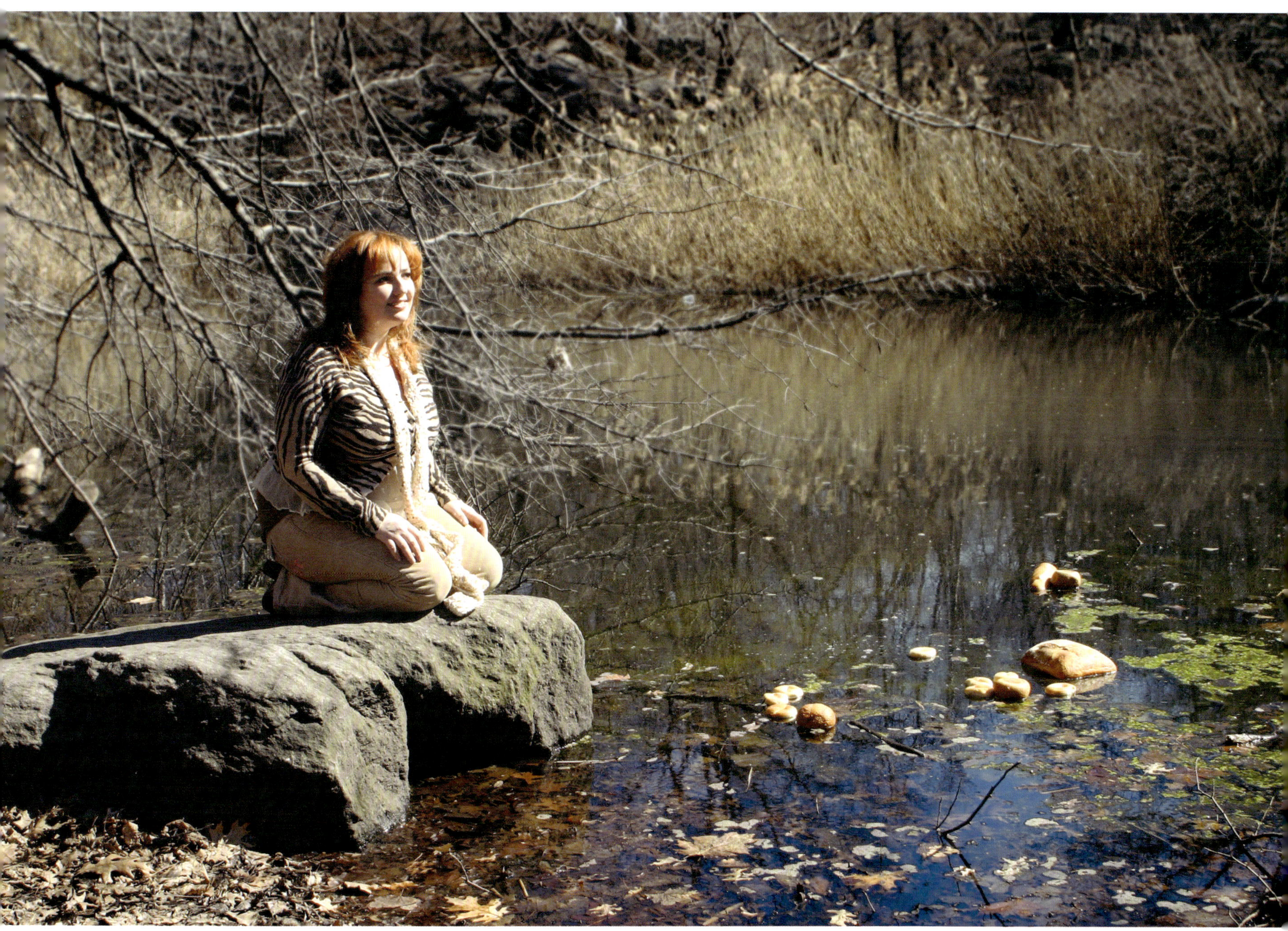

Figure 12 / *Bread on the Water* • Pages 26-27: Figure 13 / *Floating Bread* (detail)

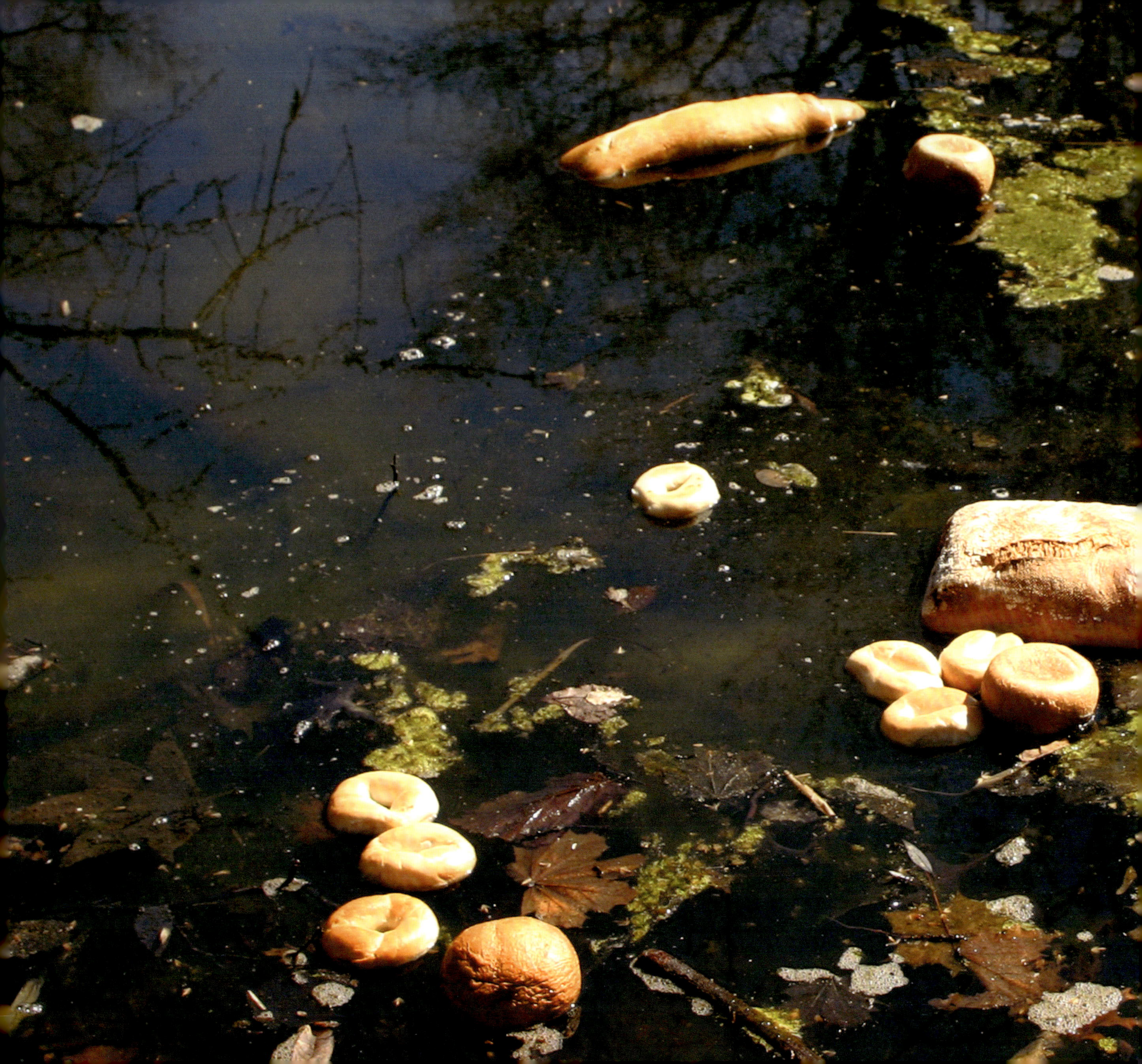

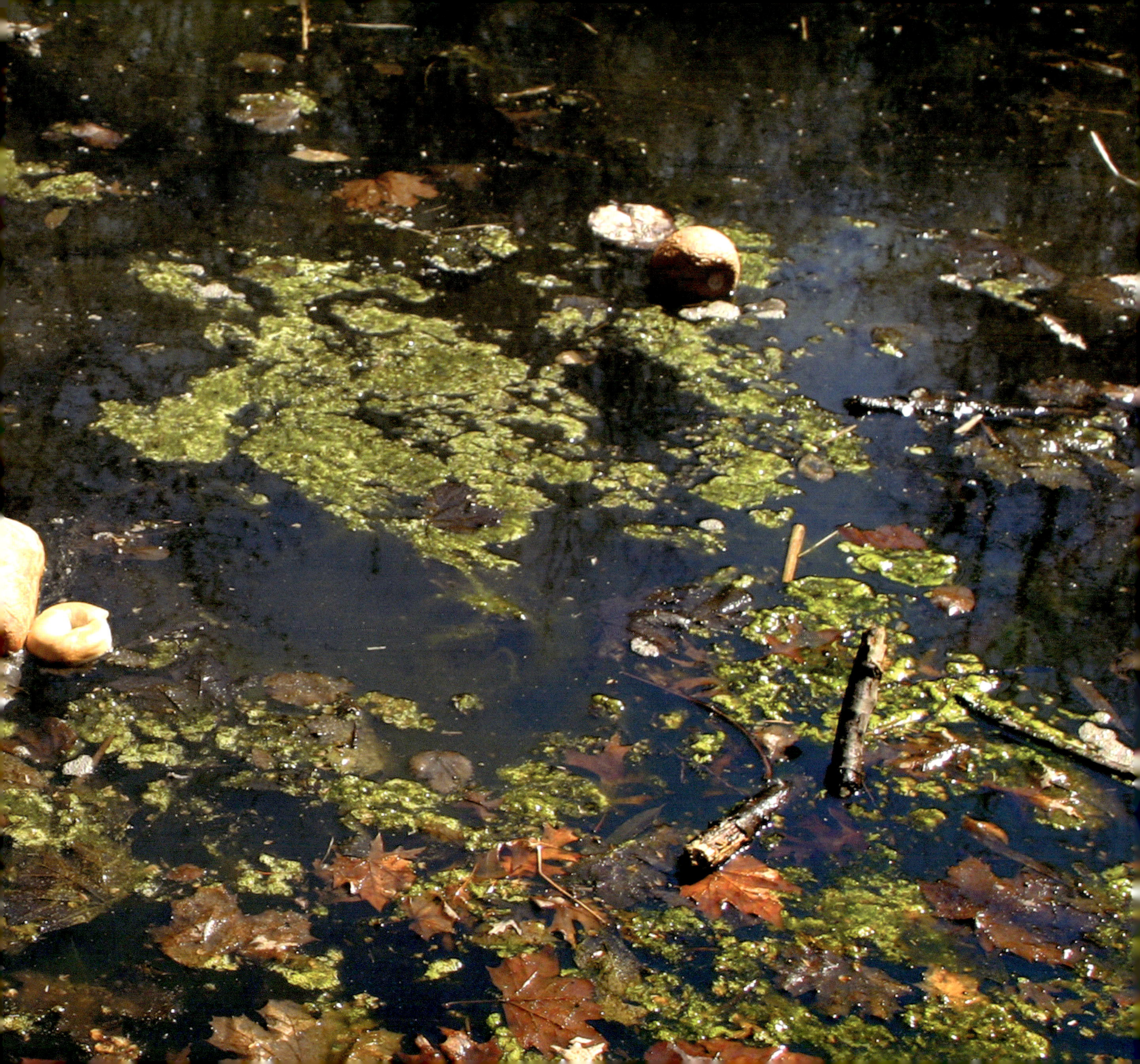

You can also coerce necessity by the waste of an opportunity. According to the rational, careerist model, such an action seems senseless, but by throwing away an opportunity, you expand possibilities that may be offered in the future. A writer who refrains from covering blank pages with text, a composer who fills a concert hall with silence—they trust that gain waste will vindicate their sacrifice.

Maurizio Cattelan buried his fiberglass sculpture *Kitakyushu 2000—New York 2004* (2004) under the floorboards of the Whitney Museum during its 2004 Biennial Exhibition. Cattelan's gesture was described as "witty" by one critic—but was it? It was gain waste, not wit, that made his piece compelling. Cattelan didn't refuse to submit a work for the show; he created a work to be buried away from sight, so that visitors would know that the work existed, but that he'd chosen to refuse to display it to the assembled, ready crowds. And this gain waste did, in fact, promote his art.

PROPITIATING WASTE

Overmuch prosperity seems to invite calamity. In propitiating waste, you induce an offsetting loss yourself, to forestall necessity from pulling accounts into balance.

The Greek historian Herodotus reported that when Amasis, King of Egypt, heard of the unbroken good fortune of Polycrates, King of Samos, he became uneasy. Amasis wrote to his fellow ruler:

> *It is a pleasure to hear of a friend and ally doing well, but . . . I cannot rejoice at your excessive prosperity. . . . I suggest that you deal with the danger of your continual successes in the following way: think of whatever it is you value most—whatever you would most regret the loss of—and throw it away: throw it right away, so that nobody can ever see it again.*

Polycrates recognized the danger. He rowed out to sea and cast his most valuable possession, a signet ring of an emerald set in gold, into the water. But he wasn't permitted to spare himself misfortune by an offering of propitiating waste; within days, servants

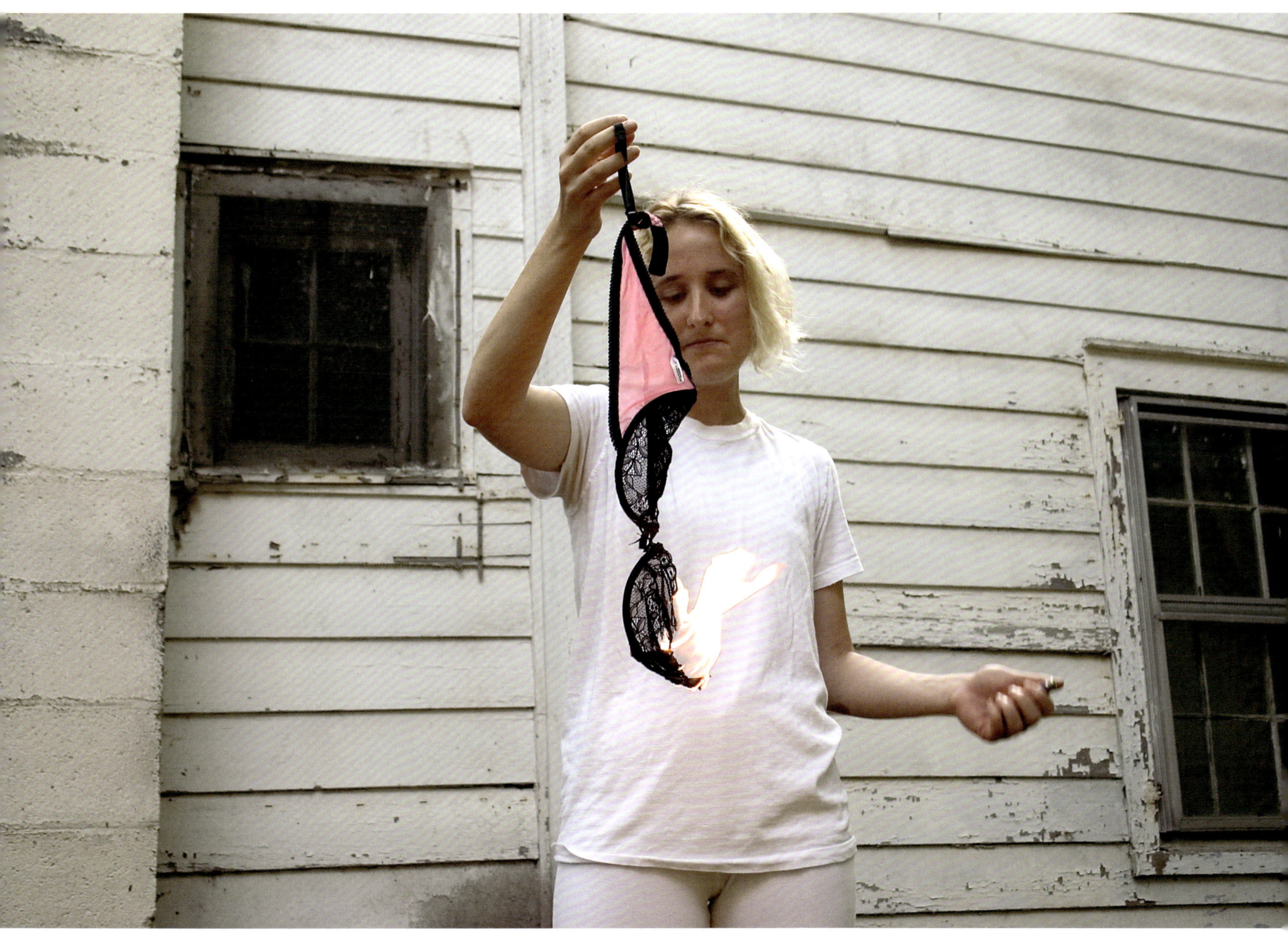

Figure 14 | *Bra Burner*

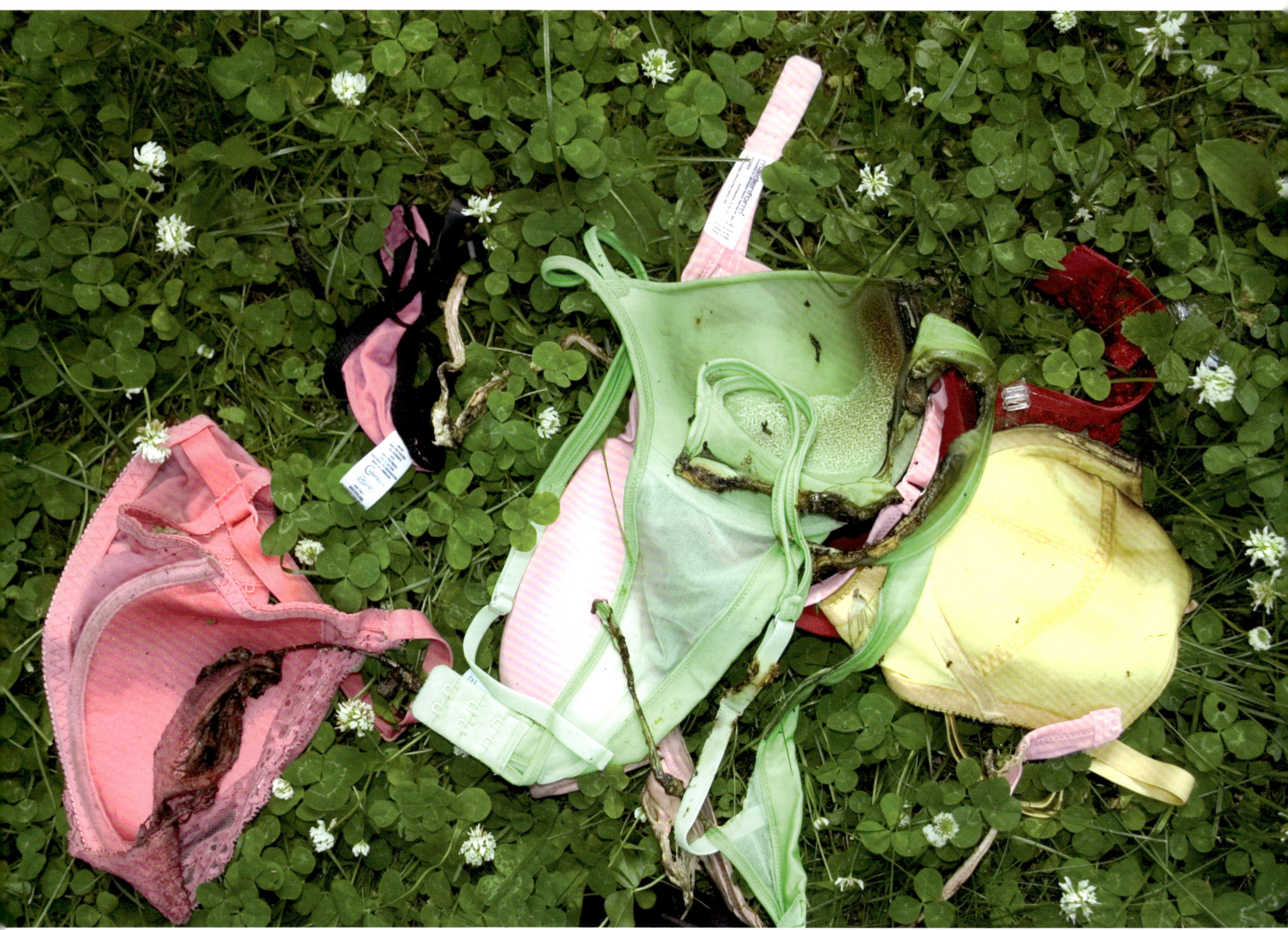

Figure 15 / *Burnt Bras*

cut open a fish given by a poor man to Polycrates and found the signet ring inside.

Divine necessity demands tribute, even now, when there are no longer any gods to receive it.

HOARD WASTE

Cabinets overflow with medicines that will expire before they can be used, or spices that will lose their flavor before they're tasted. But the thrill here is not in the waste but in the comforting hoard.

The drive for hoard waste can be so insistent that an owner will refuse to use a possession even when use wouldn't diminish it. For example, artist Joseph Cornell loved his record albums so much that he never opened them. Visitors were puzzled to see hundreds of albums, still sealed in plastic, piled in his house.

HOST WASTE

A host strives to create an air of hospitable surplus, because to have *just enough* for your guests is too meager: the wine, the platters, must overflow. Host waste is the result of pleasing profusion, and the waste is incidental.

GIFT WASTE

Although gifts sometimes seem wastefully excessive, they are in fact embedded in a tight system of equivalent exchange. Gift-givers take great care to spend precisely the appropriate amount.

STATUS WASTE

One person boards a horse but never rides; another buys season tickets to the opera but never attends. Japanese businessmen buy expensive golf clubs, even though they can't afford to play. Profane waste? No. The purpose is *association* with prestige and wealth—conspicuous consumption—not actual use, and therefore, there's been no loss or frustration of the possession.

IMMORTALIZING WASTE

Laying waste to an object of great value or endurance etches the destroyer's name in history. Herostratus—a figure much admired by Hitler—burned down the Temple of Diana in 356 B.C. to eternalize his name (and so he did). Media magnate William Randolph

Hearst traveled to Europe as a boy. When his tutor pointed out a light that had burned in Rome for a thousand years, Hearst said, "I'd like to put out that light. Isn't there some way it can be done?"

After Lee Harvey Oswald was arrested, just ninety minutes after he shot President John F. Kennedy, he told a police captain, "Everybody will know who I am now."

WITNESS WASTE

It's thrilling to watch or cause the willful destruction of a useful object, but it's not profane waste if the loss isn't the owner's.

Tarquin Winot, the narrator of John Lanchester's novel *The Debt to Pleasure*, cheerfully confides a desire to stage a spectacular disaster:

> *Who has not, on passing some large public masterpiece of architecture, or glimpsing an exquisitely ordered and human domestic interior through a ground-floor window (the sheet music open on the piano, the steepling bookcases and expectant hearth) felt an uncomplicated urge to set fire to them?*

Few would so willingly admit to the same impulse, yet riotous spectators applaud demolition derbies, and crowds gather to watch rocks smash through windows. The Duchess of Marlborough recalled a dinner where guests cheered at the tremendous crash of shattered china when a footman dropped a tray. Their host, Lord de Grey, had specially bought the china for the very purpose of delighting his guests by having it smashed. In her memoir *What Falls Away*, actress Mia Farrow recalled a time when she deposited two of her children with her then-lover Woody Allen:

> *When I returned less than an hour later,*
> *he was throwing his hats and gloves into the fire.*
> *The kids were ecstatic.*
> *"I ran out of things to do," he shrugged.*

The casinos of Las Vegas stand amid a desert—so the Bellagio Hotel Casino features an array of 1,200 choreographed outdoor fountains and a water show staged around a tank that consumes 1.5 million gallons of water, and the Mirage resort boasts a rain forest

Disneyland revive its "Electrical Parade," with its 500,000 colored light bulbs? Not seen in California for years, it returned in 2001 when California suffered a crippling shortage of electricity.

GRAB WASTE

A closet crammed with a hundred pairs of virtually identical black shoes might resemble profane waste, but it's not the same. The owner craves the buzz of the grab, and the shoes are merely the residuum.

WORTHLESS WASTE

Profane waste can't occur if the lost or frustrated possession has no value. The instant his tennis shoe fell overboard, the owner scooped up the other shoe and threw it into the water—a precise and instant recognition of the worth of the remaining shoe.

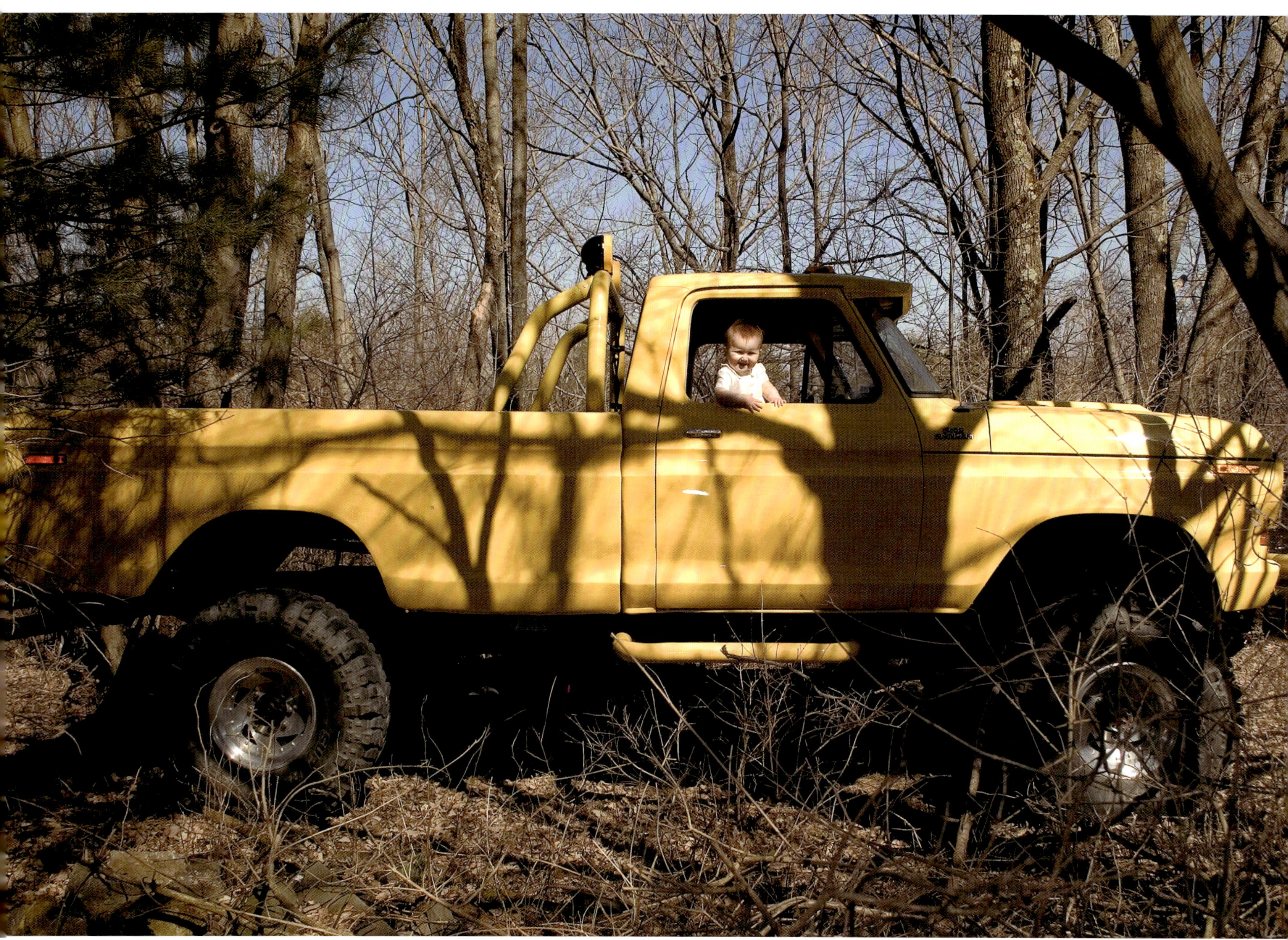

Figure 16 | *Monster Birthday*

None of these types of waste, however, qualify as profane waste.

Only heedless waste, defiant waste, and denying waste meet profane waste's exacting requirements: that the waste strike an owner's own possession, ignite a powerful emotion as a consequence of the action, and carry no expectation of return.

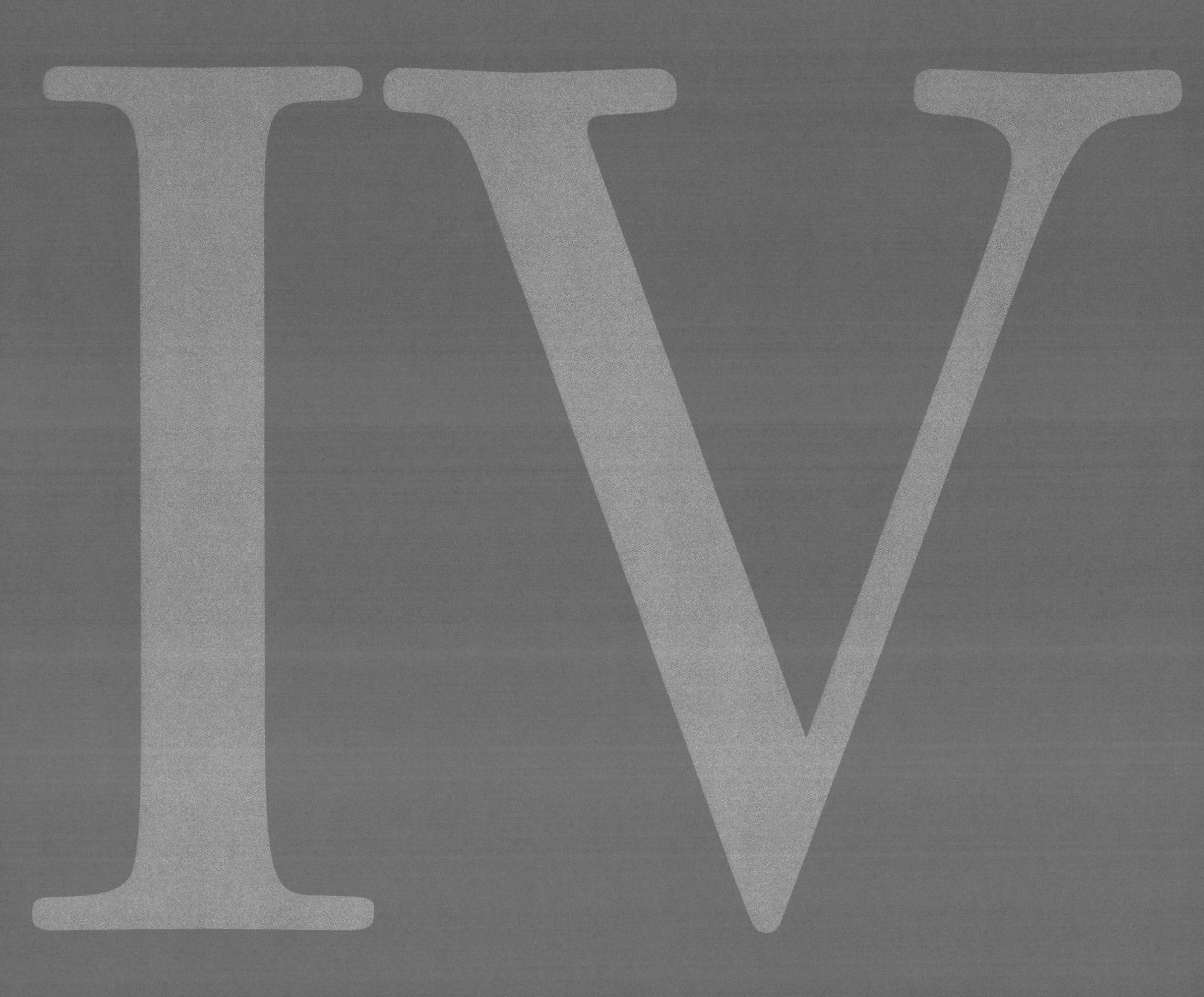

Species of Profane Waste

HEEDLESS WASTE

Heedless waste, *like all profane waste,*
declares a scorn for necessity.

You weary of economy and prudence, and long
to thwart your own avarice.

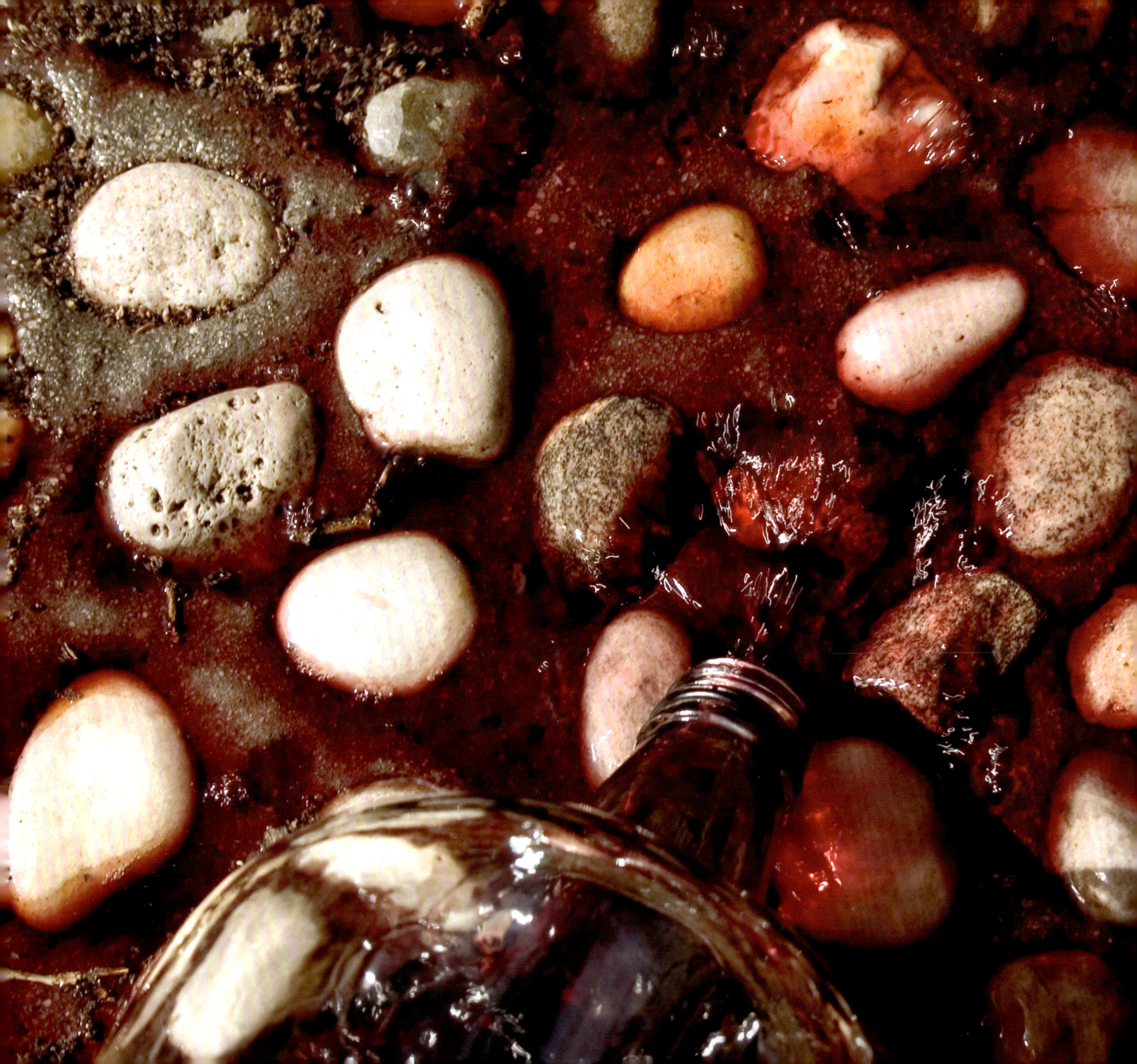

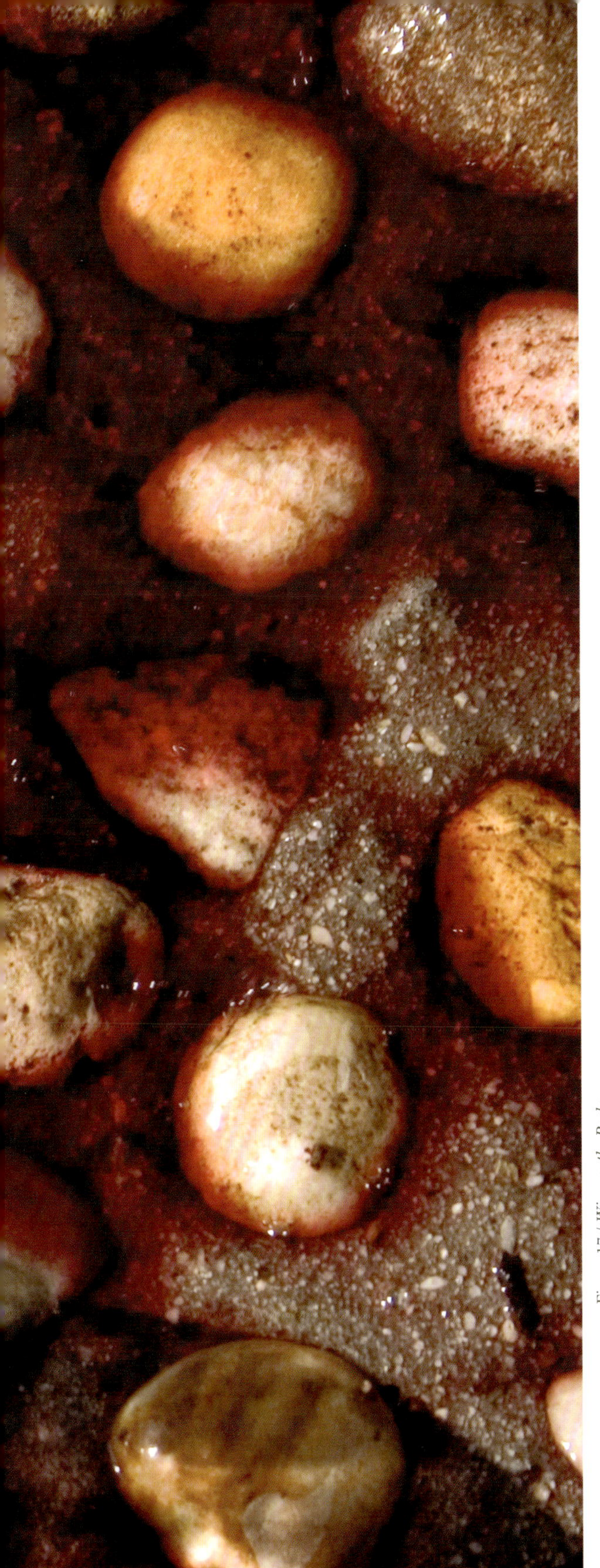

Figure 17 / *Wine on the Rocks*

Nature, despite its lavish profusion, wastes nothing. Every fallen apple or rotted fish is salvaged; every creature lays in stores for the winter. So by recklessly spending without counting the cost, by disregarding the future, you show superiority to animal practicality.

Nature does have its own forms of Veblen's conspicuous consumption. The rainbow tail of a peacock, for example, is purely for show. However, this profusion isn't really waste, because the peacock's feathers win the attention of the peahen, which is assured by the impressive display that her mate is fit and strong, and so likely to have healthy offspring.

True profane waste is an observance reserved for man.

Your heedless waste celebrates your release from the principle of balanced accounts. Others, suffocated by living within their limits, watch with a mixture of fascination and repulsion.

Heedless waste may appear careless and accidental, but it's not. For decades, a concentration camp survivor carried a sandwich in his pocket each day, and nothing gave him greater pleasure than to toss away the sandwich each night. Movie producer Don Simpson's determination to wear each of his identical pairs of Levi's only once required more effort than rotating the same few pairs of jeans. Infamous arbitrageur Ivan Boesky ordered every entrée on the menu of Café des Artistes, tasted each dish, and then sent all but one back to the kitchen.

Not only the rich indulge in heedless waste; to the contrary, poor people enjoy heedless waste as a way to create an atmosphere of plenty and expendability. One person may crash a car into a tree in a fury of possession, while another throws away a handful of carefully collected coupons. One person may overtip by five hundred dollars; another neglects to pick up a dropped pencil.

Near the end of dinner, you order another bottle of Latour, knowing that no one will drink it: you *want* to leave it behind, opened and untouched on the restaurant table, when you depart. Or you can make the same gesture by refusing to fill your water bottle from the tap but instead buying an expensive bottle of Fiji flat water—and then throwing it away full.

You spend out, ignoring the cost, and enrich yourself with contempt for riches. On a yachting trip during his brief reign, King Edward VIII drove three thousand golf balls off the deck. "I love a splash!" he declared.

Not surprisingly, food is a common object of heedless waste. In his novel *Mating*, Norman Rush describes the custom on a poor communal farm in Botswana:

> *An undeclared object . . . seemed to be for teatime to finish each day with something remaining uneaten on the table, no matter how much or how little had been provided. Everyone seemed to know what this exercise was about and to enjoy being part of it, even the children.*

Heedless waste undermines practical necessity; it is its very inefficiency and impracticality that is so gratifying. In the movie *Titanic*, Rose neither wears nor sells the diamond necklace she's kept for decades, but in the end casts it into the ocean in tribute to her long-dead lover.

By ripping goods from the system of rational value, by refusing to count costs, you illuminate values other than strict economic benefit. In the Isak Dinesen short story and movie *Babette's Feast*, after winning

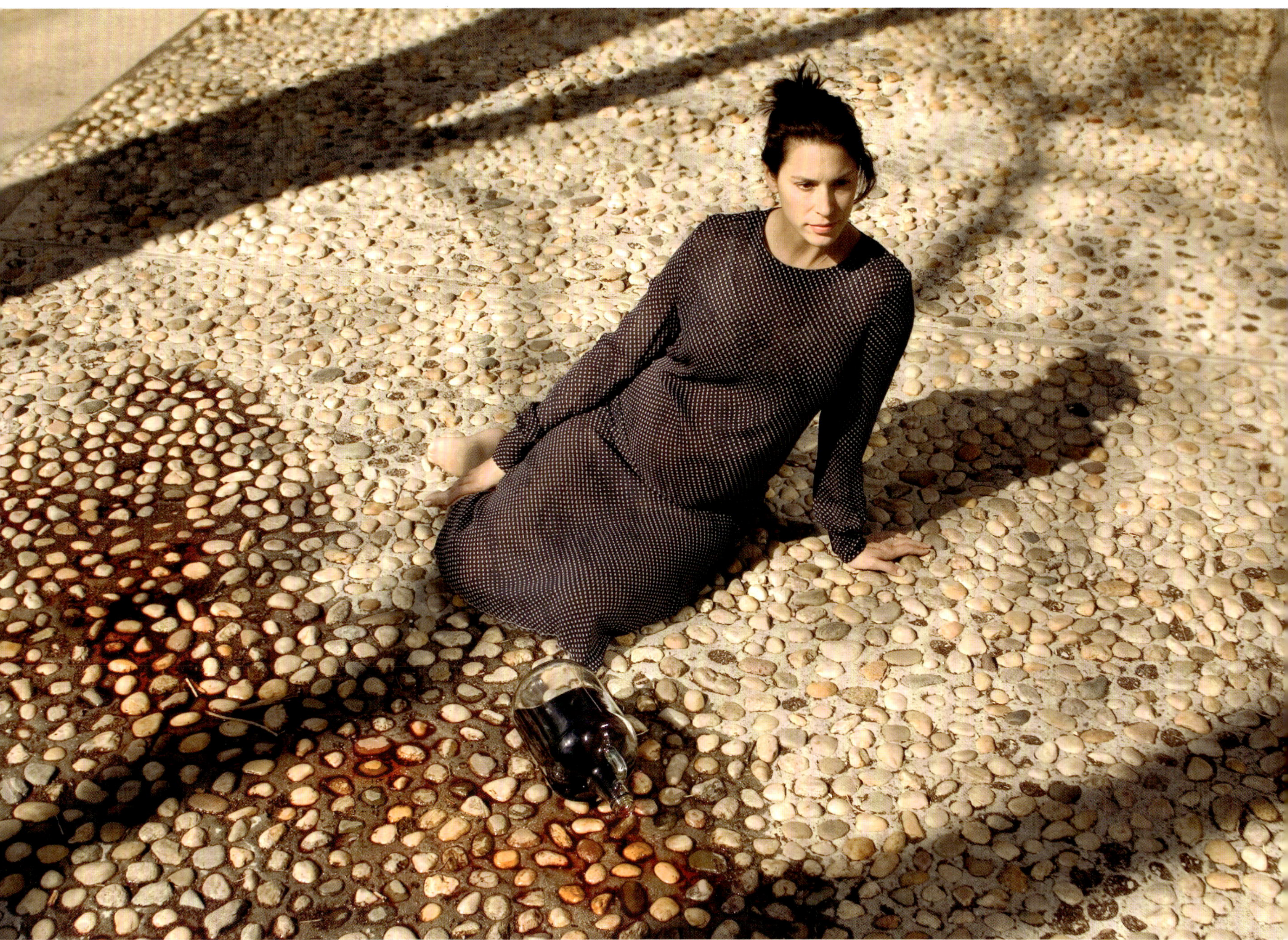

Figure 18 | *Wine Spiller*

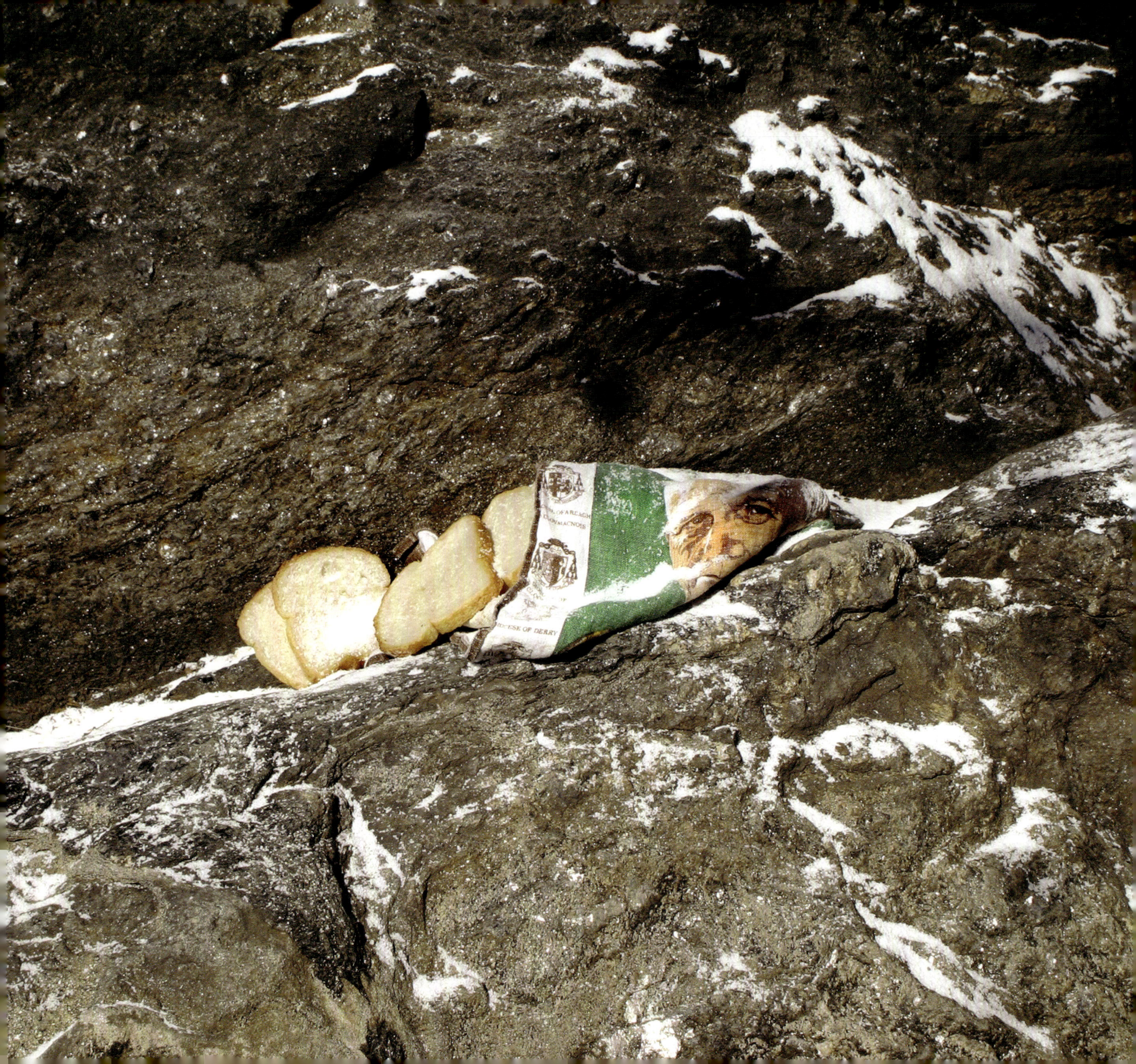
OF DERRY

the lottery, a poor servant chooses to lavish her entire new fortune on preparing a magnificent banquet of a kind never before enjoyed by her ascetic guests.

And consider that, although Jesus' disciples criticized the woman Mary for lavishing a costly ointment of spikenard on Jesus, rather than optimizing its monetary value, Jesus praised Mary for her gesture:

> *There came unto [Jesus] a woman having an alabaster box of very precious ointment, and poured it on his head, as he sat at meat.*
>
> *But when his disciples saw it, they had indignation saying, To what purpose is this waste?*
>
> *For this ointment might have been sold for much, and given to the poor. When Jesus understood it, he said unto them, Why trouble ye the woman? for she hath wrought a good work upon me.*
>
> *For ye have the poor always with you; but me ye have not always.*
>
> *For in that she hath poured this ointment on my body, she did it for my burial.*
>
> *Verily I say unto you, Wheresoever this gospel shall be preached in the whole world, there shall also this, that this woman hath done, be told for a memorial of her.*

Initially, artist Michael Landy had planned to use material left over at the end of *Break Down* to repay some of his backers with sacks of granules valued at £4,000 each, but instead, he buried all of it. If Landy had made practical use of the remains—if he'd sought some kind of return—he would have negated the power of his action.

Figure 19 / *Pope Salt Sacrifice* (detail)

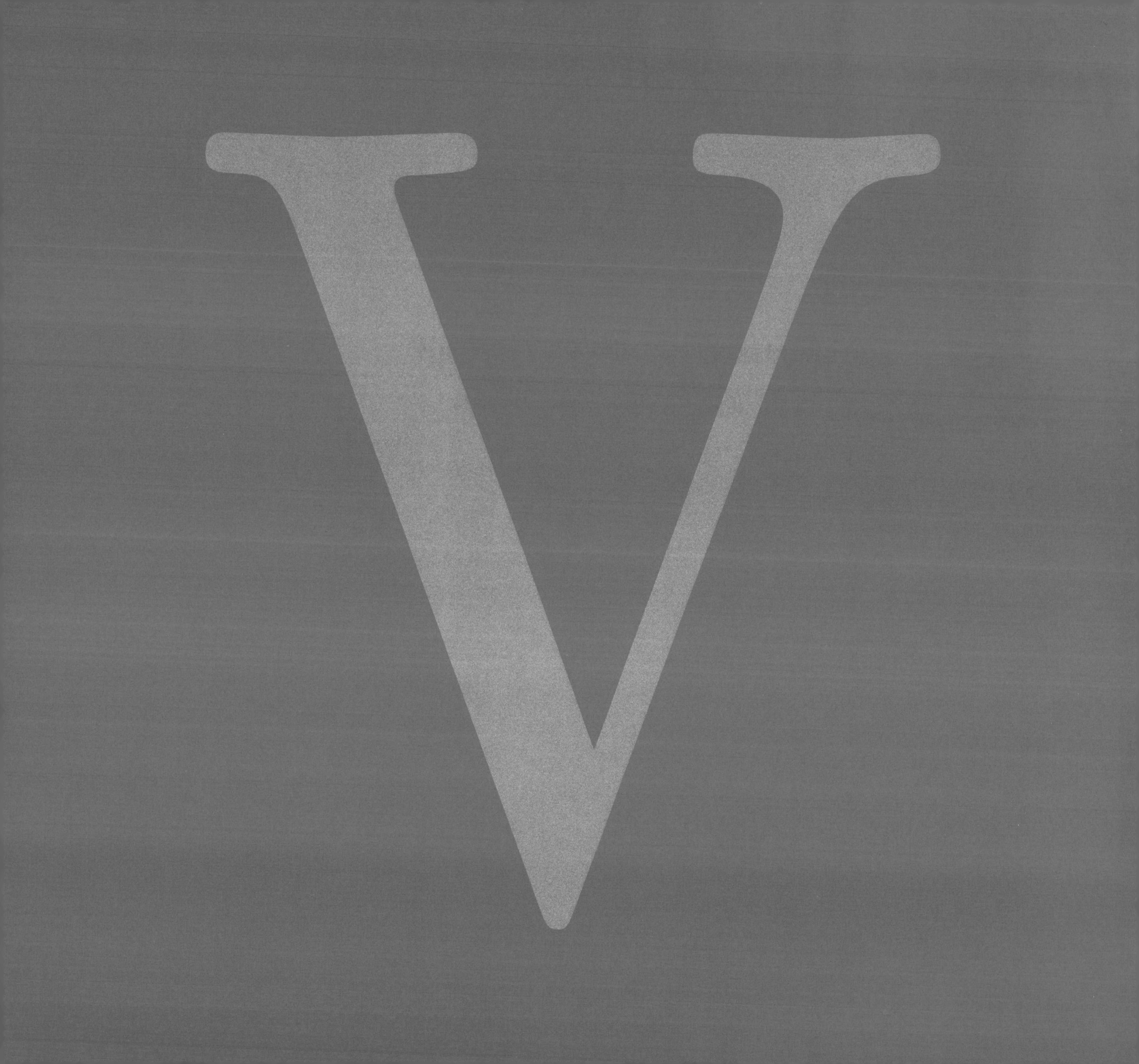

Species of Profane Waste

DEFIANT WASTE

Attachment to possessions infects the owner with the need to acquire, to cling, to protect. In defiant waste, *you show your superiority to the possessions that bind and sustain you.*

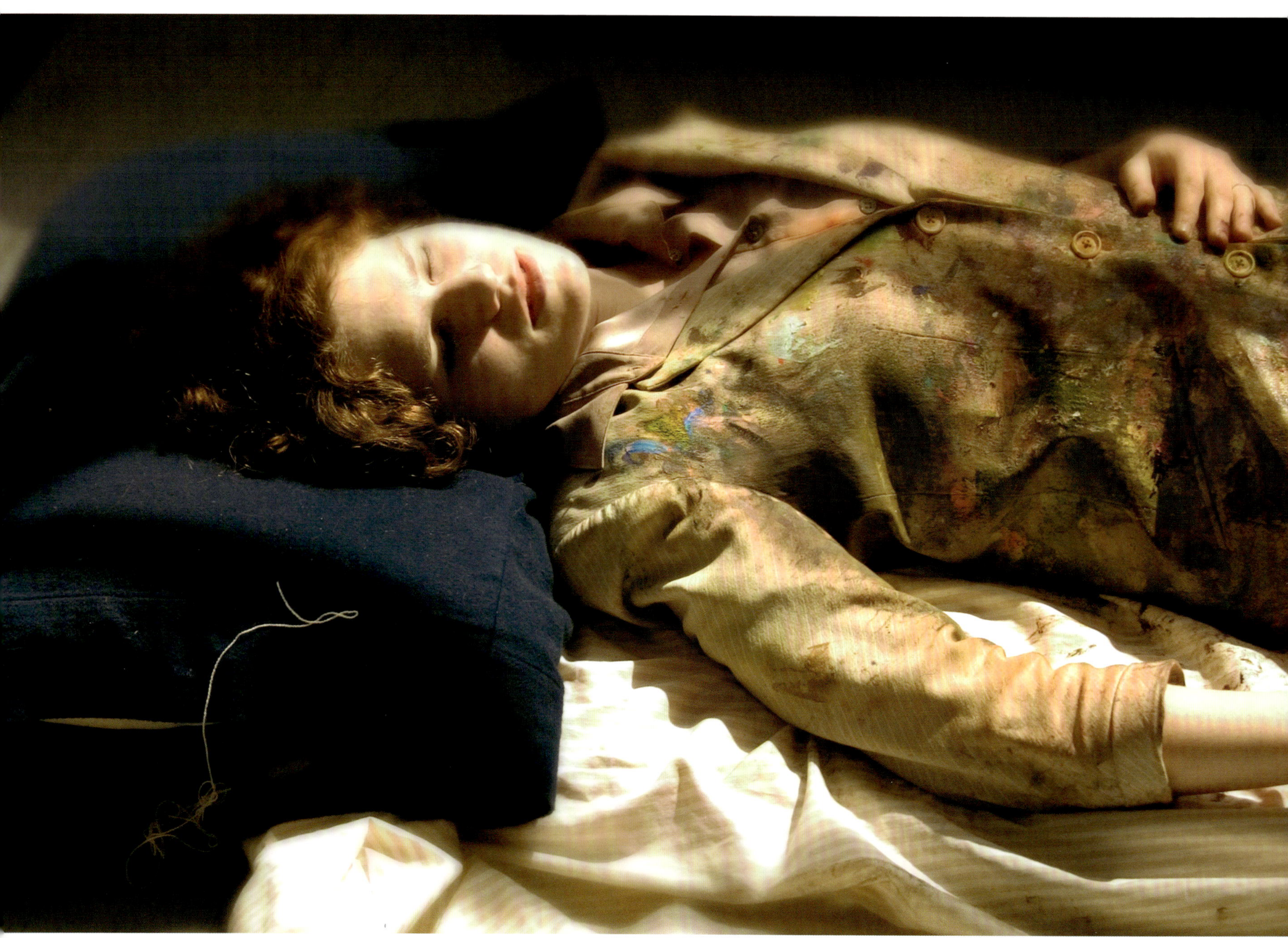

Figure 20 / *Young Painter*

Inanimate objects, with their needs and their seductions, exert a power that is generally overlooked. As literary theorist and cultural critic Elaine Scarry pointed out in her book *The Body in Pain*:

> *Perhaps no one who attends closely to artifacts is wholly free of the suspicion that they are, though not quite animate, not quite inanimate.*

Some people are particularly susceptible to the power of objects. Do you feel this? Do you crave beautiful possessions with a grasping *object lust* that drives you to acquire and collect—not from any desire to impress an audience, but from an aesthetic passion centered on the things themselves?

Collectors, in particular, suffer the exquisite pains and pleasures of object lust. Of course, people collect for other reasons as well: to indulge sheer acquisitiveness, to display their discernment, to satisfy a Medici fantasy, to launder a fortune ignominiously gained, to win entrée into Manhattan social circles, or to score a seat on a prestigious museum board. Some even hope to achieve immortality—like Frick, Guggenheim, Mellon, or Tate—by associating themselves with a collection of masterpieces gathered under their name.

Only a few of these collectors are moved by true object lust: the powerful, sensual response to objects. These collectors know the gnawing desire, the stealthy pursuit, the melancholy longing for things out of reach, and the delirious triumph of possession.

Any collector, whether of treasure or junk, confronts the objects' heavy demands—their relentless need to be protected and maintained. And so the desire to possess gives rise to the contrary urge to smash, to shred, to set things to burning. By deliberately wasting beloved possessions, you break their hold.

Sometimes these objects don't represent wealth, but are painfully precious. Their destruction would be distressing, but also liberating. In *A Heartbreaking Work of Staggering Genius*, novelist Dave Eggers considered the furniture that he kept after his parents died:

> *I try not to think of the antiques. . . . I want to save everything and preserve all this but also want it all gone. . . . Wouldn't it be something just to burn it all? Throw it in the street?*

On April 30, 1844, Henry David Thoreau, a lover of nature and an experienced outdoorsman, lit a cooking fire during a dry spell in his beloved Concord woods. A stray spark spread and set more than three hundred acres ablaze. Thoreau's journal records that he sat on a high rock to watch:

> *I said to myself . . . I have set fire to the forest. . . . I settled it with myself and stood to watch the approaching flames. It was a glorious spectacle, and I was the only one there to enjoy it.*

The destruction of something precious frees you from worries for the future. When a bombing raid near the end of the war destroyed Joseph Goebbels's Ministry for Public Enlightenment and Propaganda, Goebbels's diary described the devastation of his "lovely building" with relief as well as sorrow:

> *Now, however, we have lost not only a possession but an anxiety. In future I need no longer tremble for the Ministry.*

The greater your love for your possessions, the more choking your dread of loss, and the more, therefore, you long to be set free. In her novel *The Volcano Lover*, Susan Sontag observed:

> *Every collector-passion contains within it the fantasy of its own self-abolition. . . . Perhaps every collector has dreamed of a holocaust that will relieve him of his collection—converting all to ashes, or burying it under lava.*

With defiant waste, you assert your will rather than wait for a natural cataclysm to release you. By choosing to put an end to your possessions yourself, you will be safeguarded against their unwanted loss in the future.

The only way truly to occupy an object is to destroy it.

Defiant waste, paradoxically, intensifies your pleasure in your possession, even as you see it consumed in flames or cast into the sea. You realize the value of something by what it costs you; the greater and more meaningful the thing relinquished, the richer the reward.

The stranglehold of a fortune, too, can inspire defiant waste; money, with its exciting transmutability, exerts tremendous pressure. Young Jean-Michel Basquiat was both exhilarated and disturbed by his art world success. He defied his new wealth by tossing a hundred dollars in one-dollar bills from limousine windows to panhandlers, and by messily painting in expensive designer suits.

Intoxicated with riches, the New Money moguls of the 1920s flashed cigarettes wrapped, and designed to be smoked, in hundred-dollar bills. Stuart Holzman spent ten years driving a bus in New Jersey to satisfy the condition imposed by his uncle's will: to inherit nearly fifty million dollars, Holzman was required to hold a steady job until he turned thirty-five years old. Holzman celebrated by destroying the very resource he had anticipated so long—by flinging hundred-dollar bills off of a speedboat into the ocean. Before, the money had controlled him; now, he controlled the money. (In profane waste, as elsewhere, the number "one hundred" has a peculiar fascination.)

Or, instead of destroying money outright to flout your freedom, you substitute an object that is synonymous with wealth. During a stay at the Paris Ritz, singer Mariah Carey and her boyfriend ordered 150 bottles of Cristal champagne. They drank one bottle and poured 149 bottles into the tub. Musicians Pete Townsend and Jimi Hendrix each made a show of

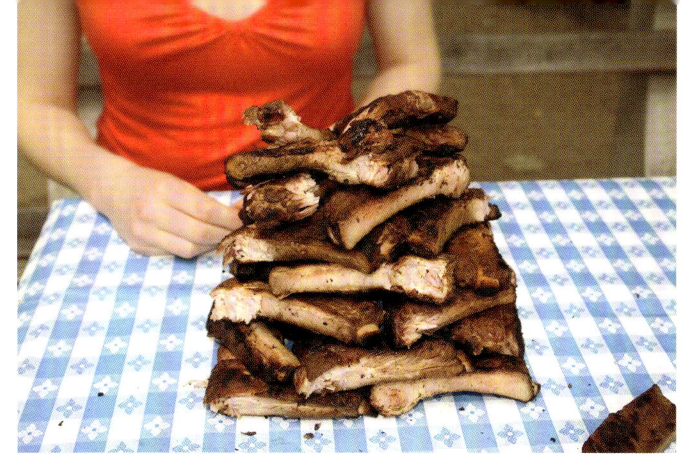

Figure 21 / *Bonehouse*

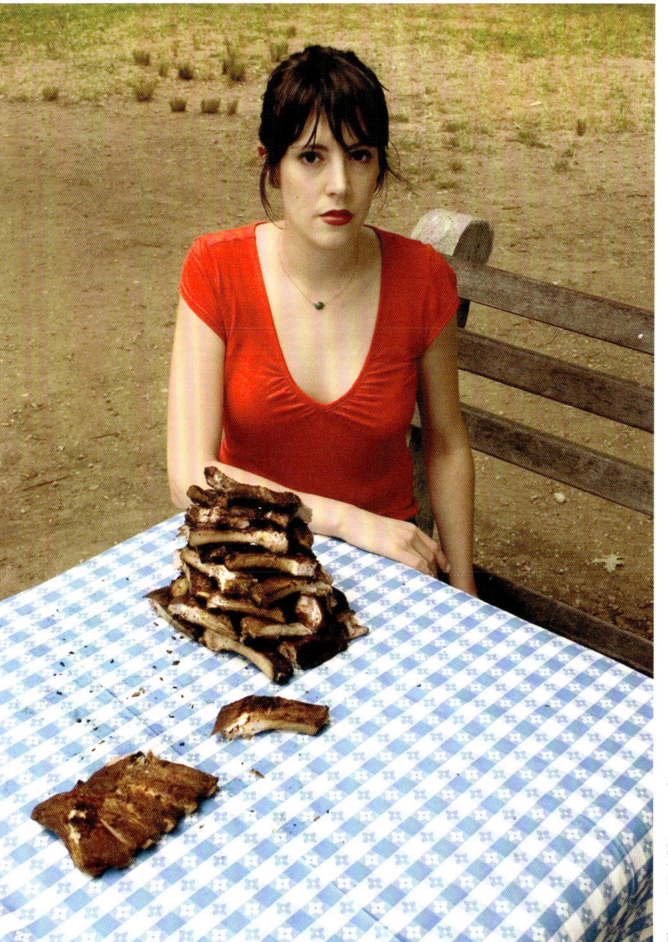

Figure 22 / *Housemaker*

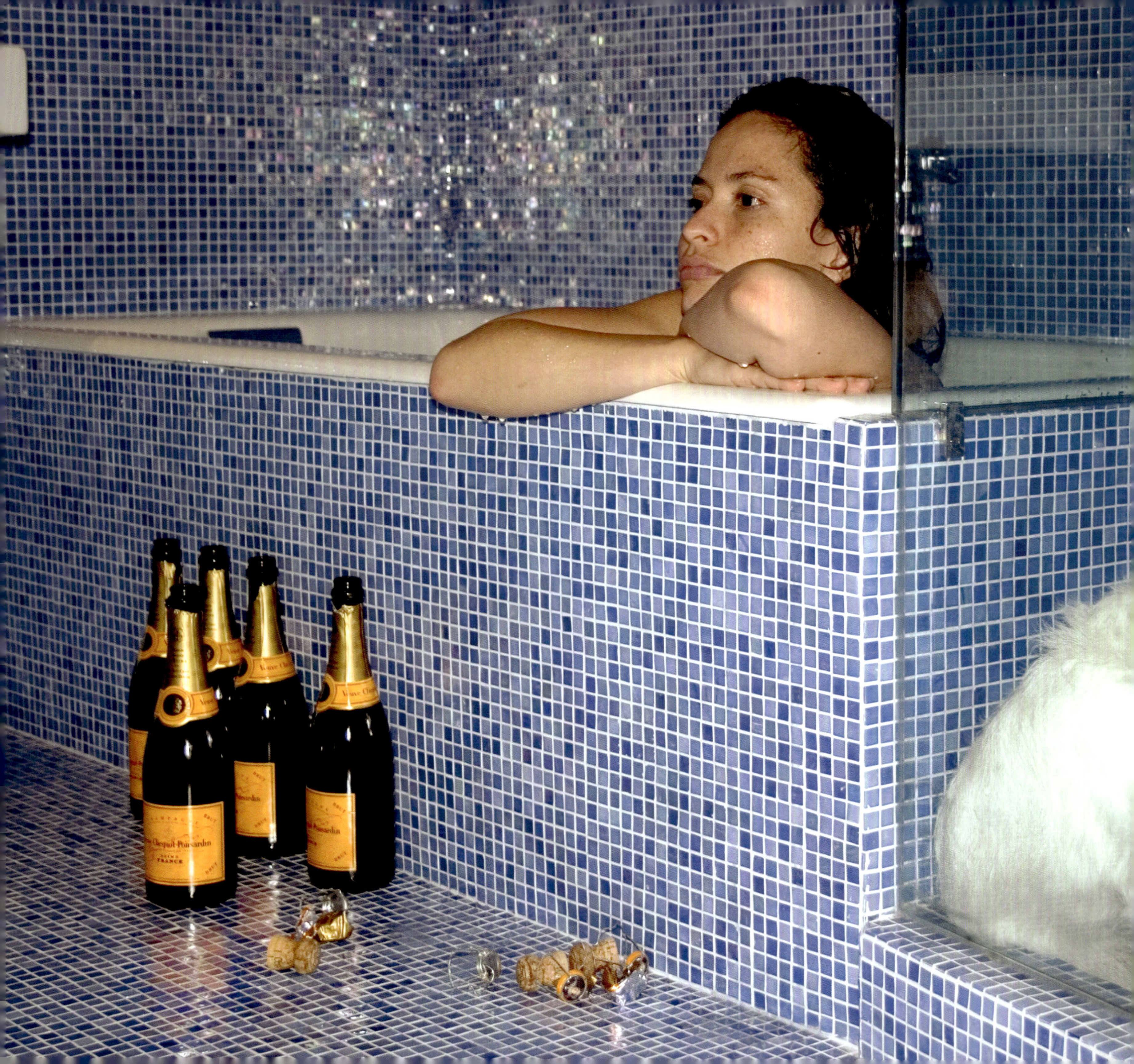
BRUT
FRANCE

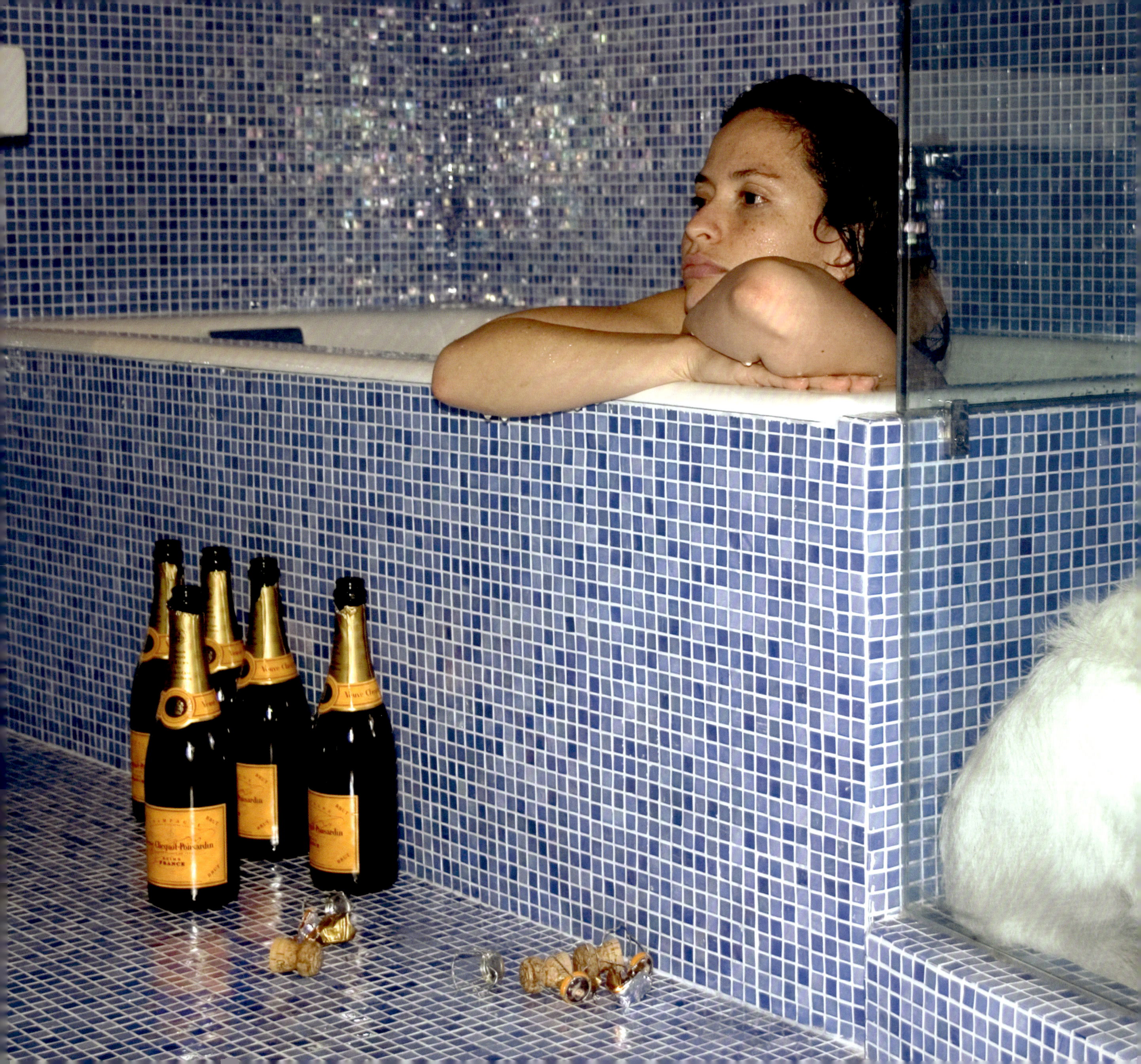

BRUT
FRANCE

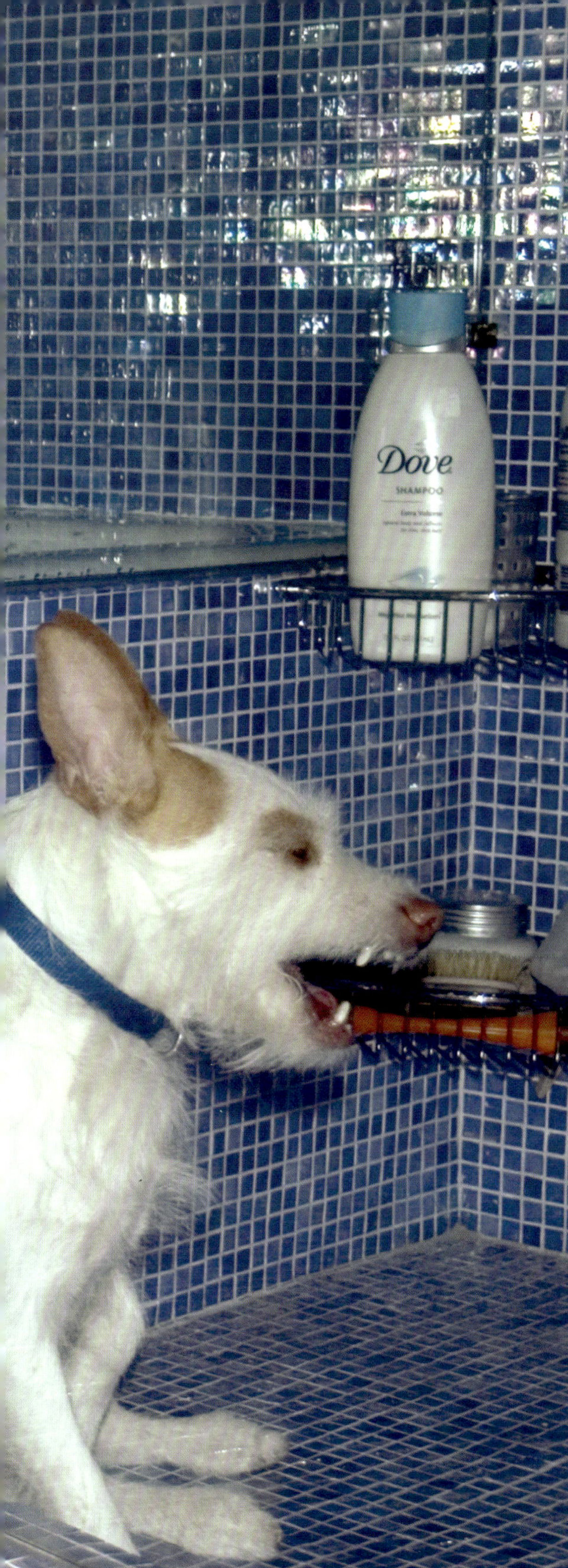

Figure 23 / *Champagne Bath* (detail)

attacking a guitar—the instruments of their success—in a frenzy of destruction.

Of all possessions, the body is the first and the most fundamental, and its claims also give rise to the impulse of defiant waste. Ascetics waste their bodies through exertion, deliberate infliction of pain, contortionism, or the renunciation of fundamental human functions such as speech, sex, or sleep—expressions of the owner's defiance of the body's demands. Anorexics, too, seek to break the relentless hold of the body and its hungers. They throw away their physical health and fertility by starving themselves—and they literally *waste away*. (As noted, food, like gold, is often present at episodes of profane waste.)

> How else do people waste their own bodies? They *get wasted* and, by intoxication, squander the body's resources of energy and health.

Perhaps it's profane waste that explains the excited interest that drunkenness so inexplicably provokes.

Any action in defiance of the body, and the wearisome need to protect and serve it, strikes deeply. Conceptual artist Chris Burden won instant fame with his 1971 performance piece, *Shoot*, in which he arranged to be shot in the left arm at short range. People found this deliberate abandonment of ordinary self-preservation to be enormously exciting.

In Virginia Woolf's novel *Mrs. Dalloway*, Clarissa Dalloway hears news of a suicide: a man had thrown himself from a window. She thinks:

> *She had once thrown a shilling into the Serpentine, never anything more. But he had flung it away. . . . A thing there was that mattered; a thing, wreathed about with chatter, defaced, obscured in her own life, let drop every day in corruption, lies, chatter. This he had preserved. . . .*
>
> *She felt glad that he had done it; thrown it away.*

Mrs. Dalloway had never done more than throw a coin into a river, but she recognized the meaning of the stranger's last spectacular gesture of defiant waste.

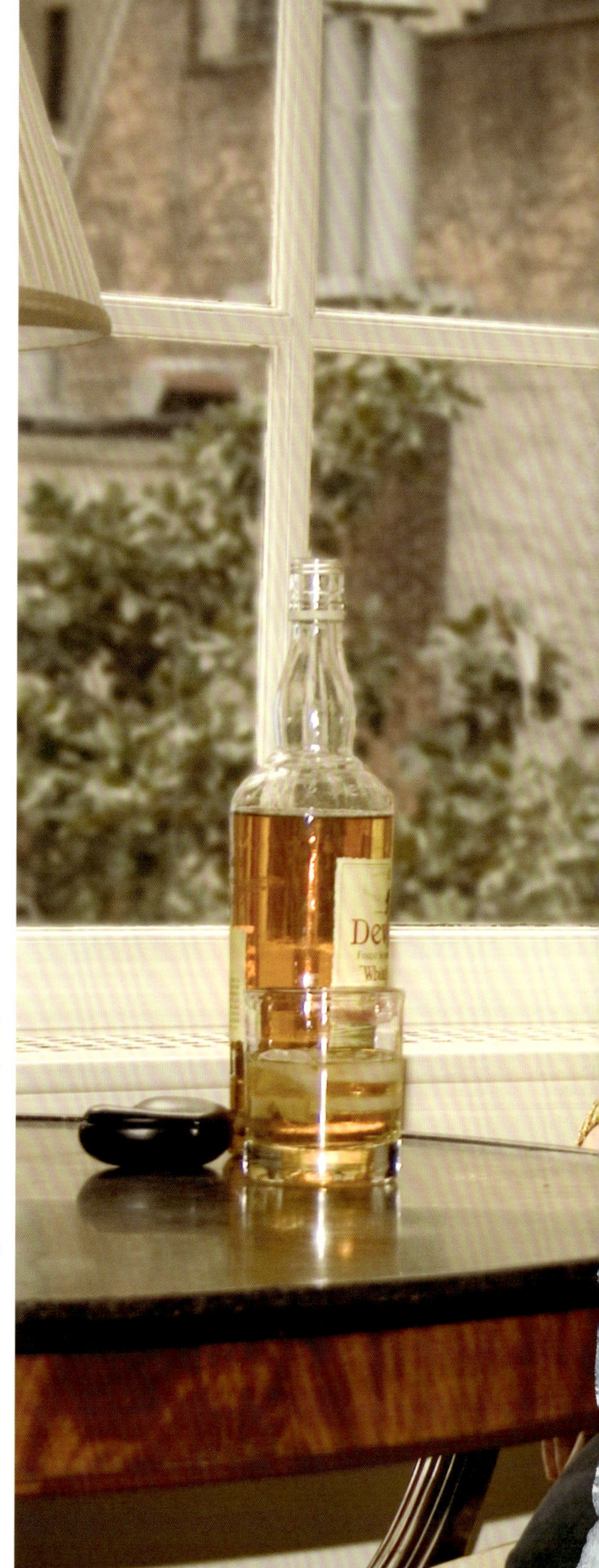

Figure 24 / *Dewar's Mother* (detail)

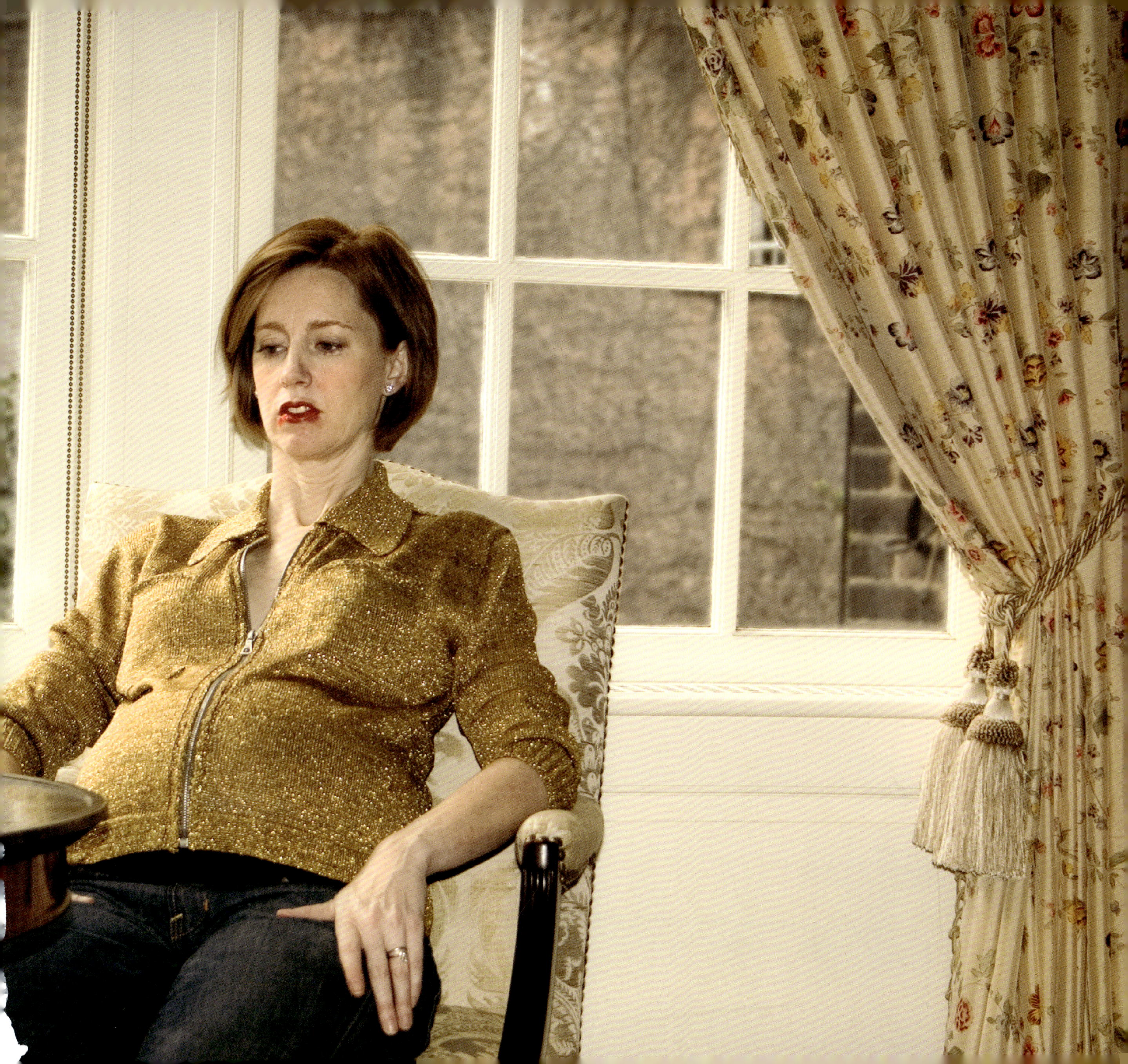

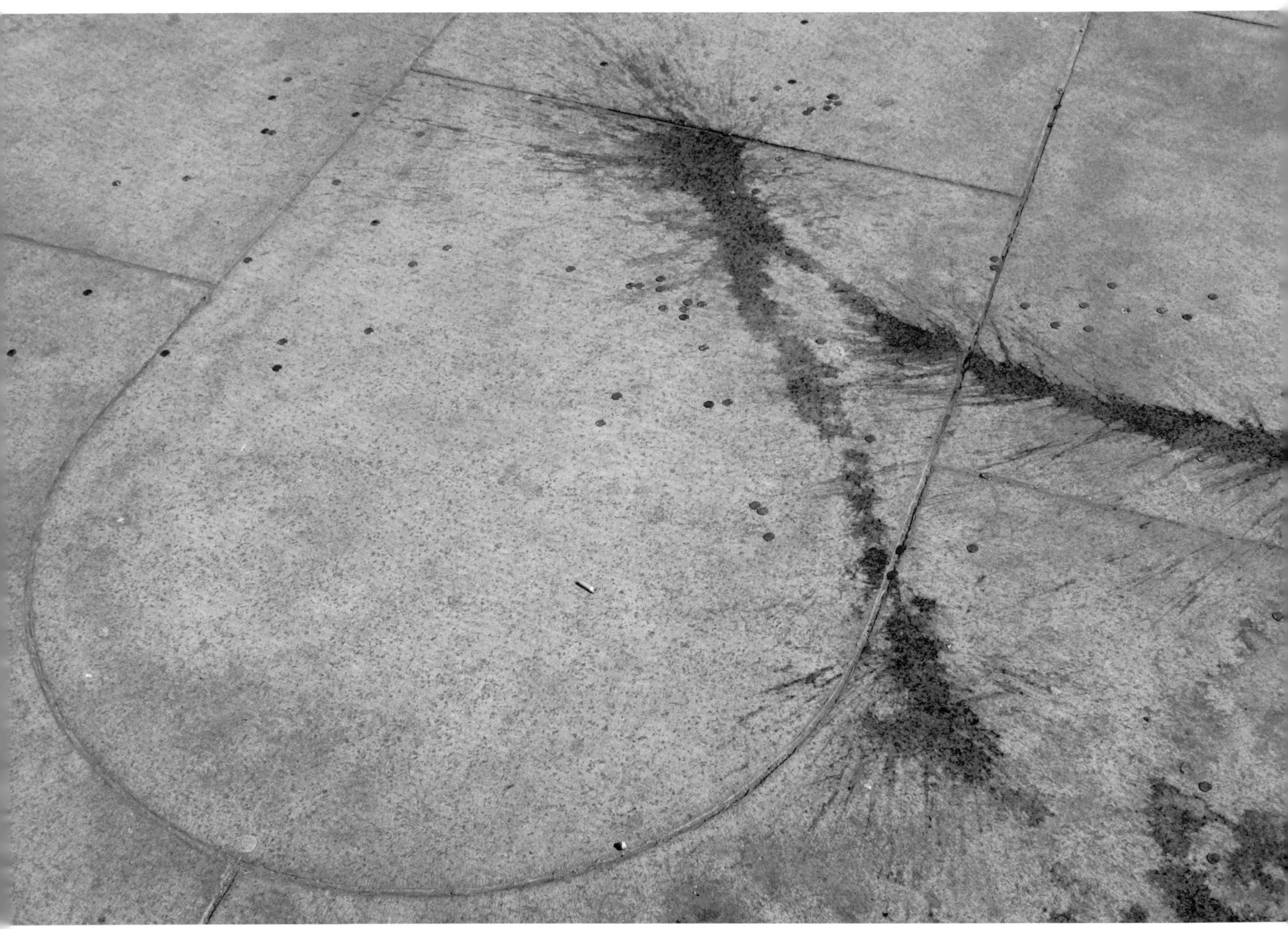

Figure 25 / *Just Pennies*

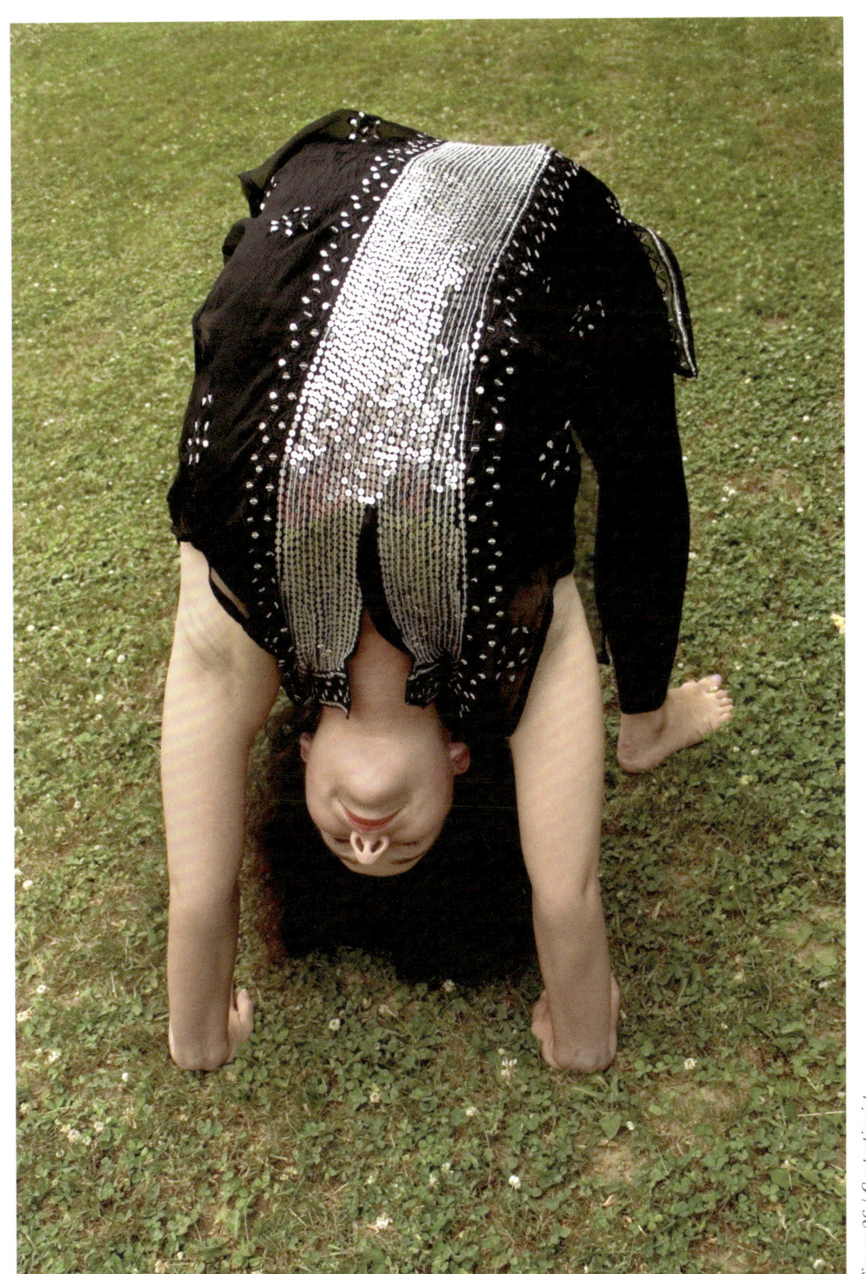

Figure 26 | *Contortionist*

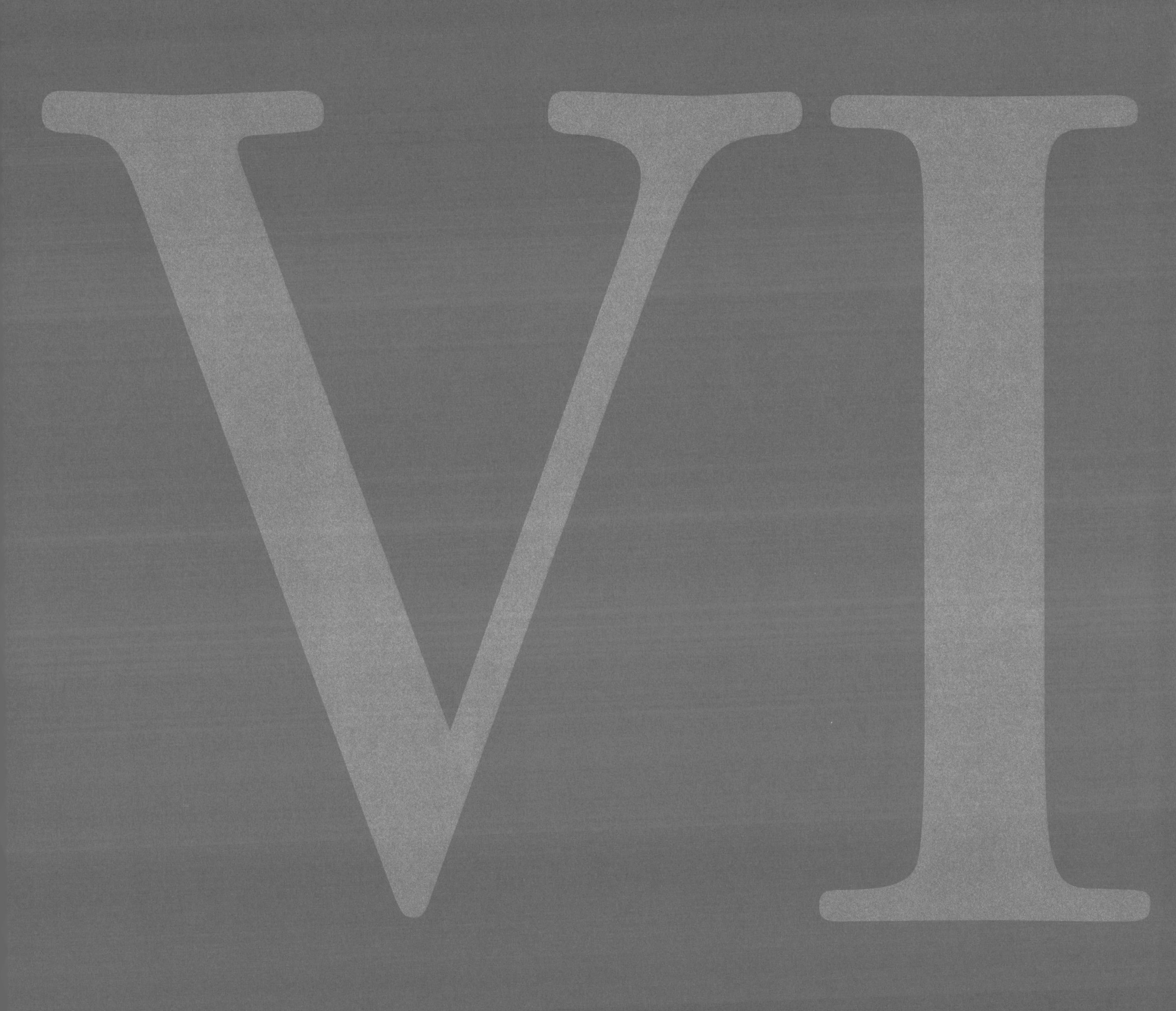
VI

Species of Profane Waste

DENYING WASTE

The only way to keep your control over an object forever is to destroy it, because otherwise it will fall into other hands. In denying waste, *you waste your possessions rather than see others enjoy them or mistreat them.*

Deranged tycoon Howard Hughes put doctors on retainer and forced them to sit idle—he had no need for their care but didn't want anyone else to benefit from their services, either. One Saudi royal family bought Italian-designed furniture for a wedding, and afterward ordered all the pieces destroyed, to make sure that no one else ever used them. Although custom requires that servants be permitted to eat leftovers lest meals be wasted, some employers instead order that all remnants be thrown away.

W. Somerset Maugham's novel *The Moon and Sixpence* tells the story of artist Charles Strickland. On his deathbed, Strickland makes his lover promise to burn his greatest work rather than allow it to survive him. Strickland's doctor reflects later:

> *I think Strickland knew it was a masterpiece. He had achieved what he wanted. . . . He had made a world and saw that it was good. Then, in pride and contempt, he destroyed it.*

Some owners don't pursue denying waste while they live, but—in a cheat—seek its gratifications by arranging for it to be carried out after their deaths. Japan's Ryoei Saito bought a Van Gogh and a Renoir for 160 million dollars. He announced that upon his death he wanted the paintings cremated along with him; only the art world's outrage forced him to change his plans.

Some owners write wills ordering the destruction of their property, to stop others from enjoying their possessions after they've died. One testator directed in her will that her valuable jewelry be buried with her body; another ordered the demolishment of his two houses; another directed his executor to destroy all money and evidences of credit belonging to his estate. But though these owners sought the satisfaction of denying waste without suffering the personal loss that it requires, they were thwarted; the societal condemnation of profane waste is too great. Courts hold these denying-waste provisions to be invalid on the grounds of "capriciousness" or as contrary to public policy.

By destroying something, you keep hold of it even after death. In Elias Canetti's novel *Auto-da-Fé*, after the book-obsessed scholar Peter Kien is driven out of his beloved library, his anxiety about its fate torments him. He returns to set his collection ablaze—and with it, himself. He truly takes possession of his books as they burn with him in an ecstasy of conflagration.

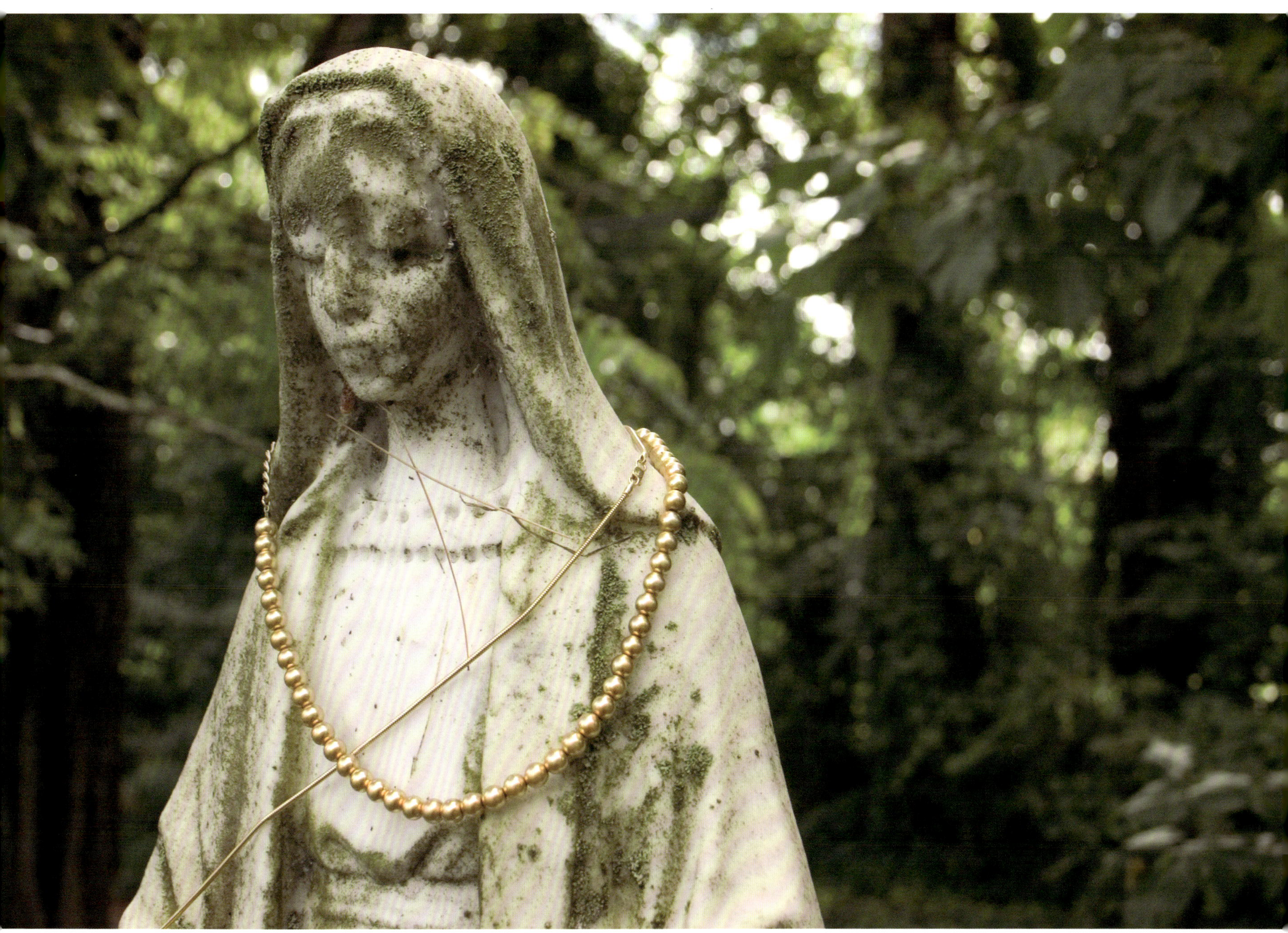

Figure 27 | *Death Gift*

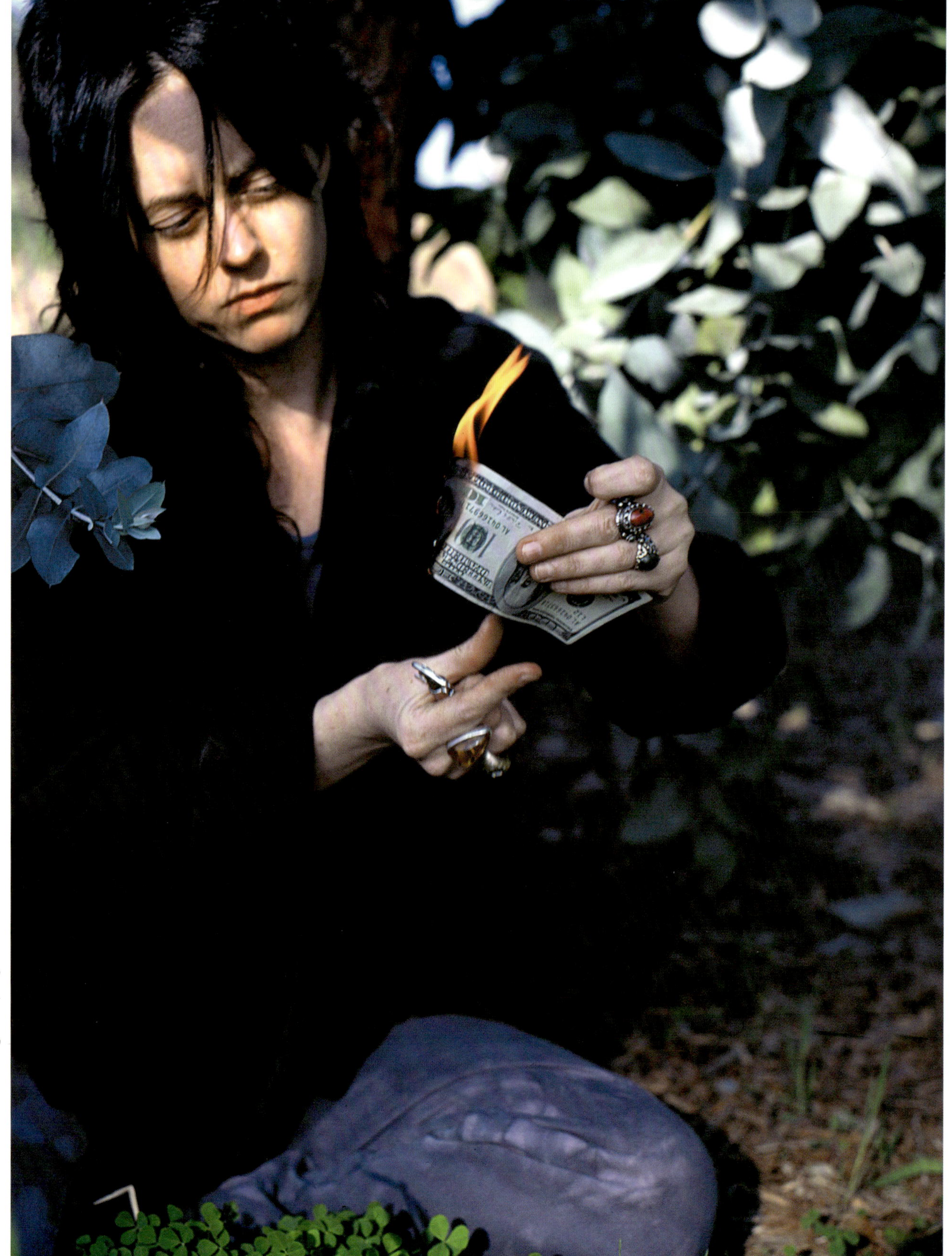

Figure 28 / *Profane Waste*

Conclusion

Frustrated by your dependence on necessary possessions, resentful of their hold on your imagination, you struggle to free yourself. How?

Profane Waste.

Caution dissolves. Liberated, powerful, you cast your possession into the fire.

Dana Hoey

Dana Hoey has a B.A. in philosophy from Wesleyan University and an M.F.A. in photography from Yale University. She has exhibited in galleries and museums in New York and Europe, including a solo show at the Hirshhorn Museum in Washington, D.C. Her work is represented by Friedrich Petzel Gallery, New York, and she teaches in the interdisciplinary M.F.A. Program at Columbia University.

Gretchen Rubin

Gretchen Rubin is the author of *Forty Ways to Look at JFK*, *Forty Ways to Look at Winston Churchill*, and *Power Money Fame Sex: A User's Guide*. She graduated from Yale College and Yale Law School and was editor-in-chief of the *Yale Law Journal*. She clerked on the U.S. Supreme Court for Justice Sandra Day O'Connor and has taught at Yale Law School and Yale School of Management. Her website is www.gretchenrubin.com.

Figure 29 / *Turkey Scratch* (detail)

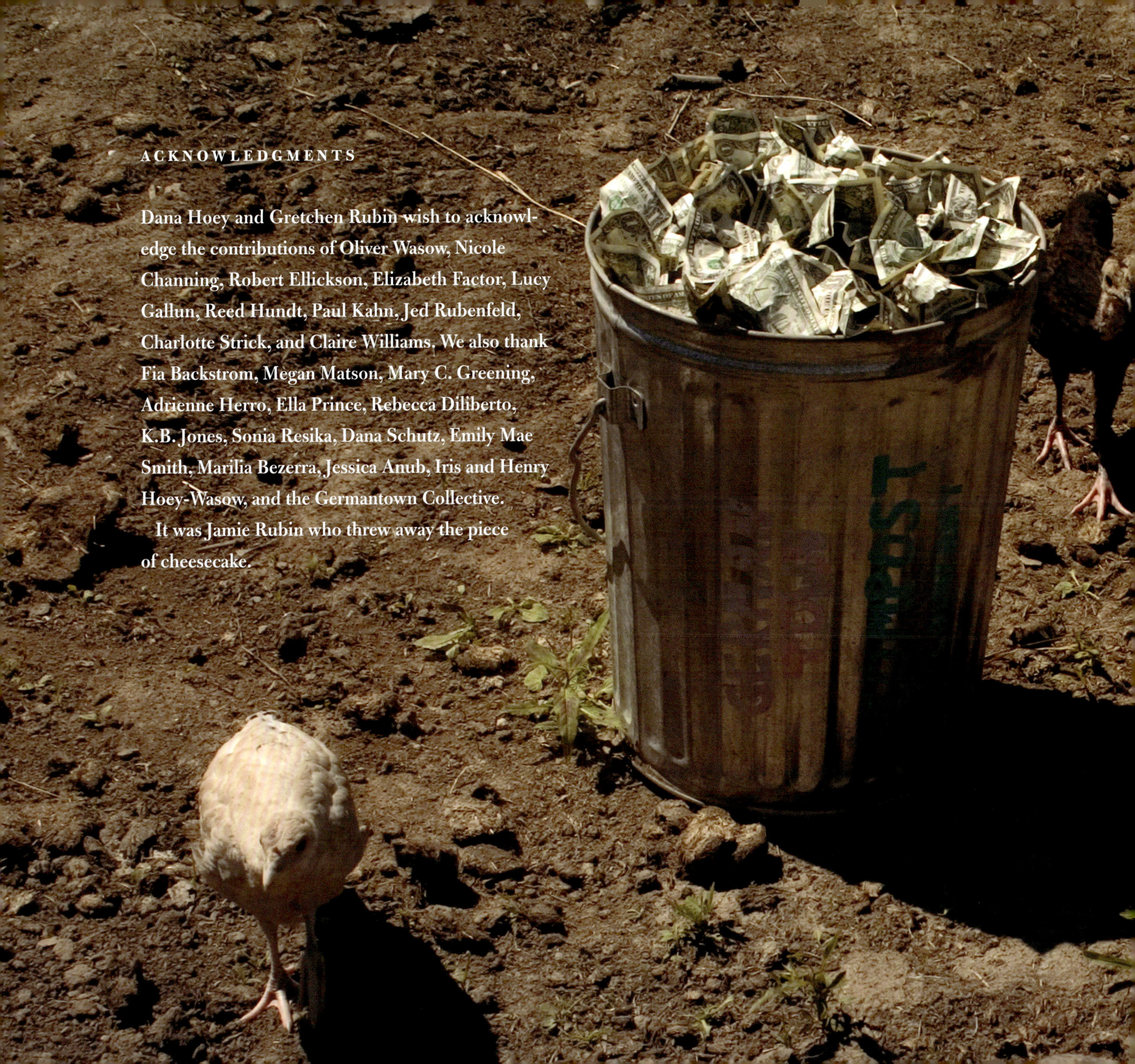

ACKNOWLEDGMENTS

Dana Hoey and Gretchen Rubin wish to acknowledge the contributions of Oliver Wasow, Nicole Channing, Robert Ellickson, Elizabeth Factor, Lucy Gallun, Reed Hundt, Paul Kahn, Jed Rubenfeld, Charlotte Strick, and Claire Williams. We also thank Fia Backstrom, Megan Matson, Mary C. Greening, Adrienne Herro, Ella Prince, Rebecca Diliberto, K.B. Jones, Sonia Resika, Dana Schutz, Emily Mae Smith, Marilia Bezerra, Jessica Anub, Iris and Henry Hoey-Wasow, and the Germantown Collective.

It was Jamie Rubin who threw away the piece of cheesecake.

LIST OF WORKS

Cover: *Frozen Cigarettes*, 2006
Archival Inkjet Print, 13 x 19 inches, Edition of 6

Endpapers: *$ in Shit*, 2005
Archival Inkjet Print, 19 x 13 inches, Edition of 6

Fig. 1: *The View,* 2005
Archival Inkjet Print, 13 x 19 inches, Edition of 6

Fig. 2: *Compost*, 2005
Archival Inkjet Print, 19 x 13 inches, Edition of 6

Fig. 3: *Pregnant Smoker 2*, 2001
Archival Inkjet Print, 13 x 19 inches, Edition of 6

Fig. 4: *Upgrade*, 2005
Archival Inkjet Print, 13 x 19 inches, Edition of 6

Fig. 5: *Hot Tea*, 2005
Archival Inkjet Print, 13 x 13 inches, Edition of 6

Fig. 6: *Storage*, 2005
Archival Inkjet Print, 13 x 19 inches, Edition of 6

Fig. 7: *Empty Fountain*, 2005
Archival Inkjet Print, 13 x 19 inches, Edition of 6

Fig. 8: *Spent Out*, 2005
Archival Inkjet Print, 13 x 19 inches, Edition of 6

Fig. 9: *Sweet 11*, 2005
Archival Inkjet Print, 13 x 19 inches, Edition of 6

Fig. 10: *Pig Food*, 2005
Archival Inkjet Print, 13 x 19 inches, Edition of 6

Fig. 11: *Reverse Ready Made*, 2005
Archival Inkjet Print, 13 x 19 inches, Edition of 6

Fig. 12: *Bread on the Water*, 2005
Archival Inkjet Print, 13 x 19 inches, Edition of 6

Fig. 13: *Floating Bread*, 2005
Archival Inkjet Print, 13 x 19 inches, Edition of 6

Fig. 14: *Bra Burner*, 2005
Archival Inkjet Print, 13 x 19 inches, Edition of 6

Fig. 15: *Burnt Bras*, 2005
Archival Inkjet Print, 13 x 19 inches, Edition of 6

Fig. 16: *Monster Birthday*, 2005
Archival Inkjet Print, 13 x 19 inches, Edition of 6

Fig. 17: *Wine on the Rocks*, 2005
Archival Inkjet Print, 13 x 19 inches, Edition of 6

Fig. 18: *Wine Spiller*, 2005
Archival Inkjet Print, 13 x 19 inches, Edition of 6

Fig. 19: *Pope Salt Sacrifice*, 2005
Archival Inkjet Print, 13 x 19 inches, Edition of 6

Fig. 20: *Young Painter*, 2005
Archival Inkjet Print, 13 x 19 inches, Edition of 6

Fig. 21: *Bonehouse*, 2005
Archival Inkjet Print, 13 x 19 inches, Edition of 6

Fig. 22: *Housemaker*, 2005
Archival Inkjet Print, 19 x 13 inches, Edition of 6

Fig. 23: *Champagne Bath*, 2005
Archival Inkjet Print, 13 x 19 inches, Edition of 6

Fig. 24: *Dewar's Mother*, 2005
Archival Inkjet Print, 13 x 19 inches, Edition of 6

Fig. 25: *Just Pennies*, 2005
Archival Inkjet Print, 13 x 19 inches, Edition of 6

Fig. 26: *Contortionist*, 2005
Archival Inkjet Print, 19 x 13 inches, Edition of 6

Fig. 27: *Death Gift*, 2005
Archival Inkjet Print, 13 x 19 inches, Edition of 6

Fig. 28: *Profane Waste*, 2001
Archival Inkjet Print, 19 x 13 inches, Edition of 6

Fig. 29: *Turkey Scratch*, 2005
Archival Inkjet Print, 13 x 19 inches, Edition of 6

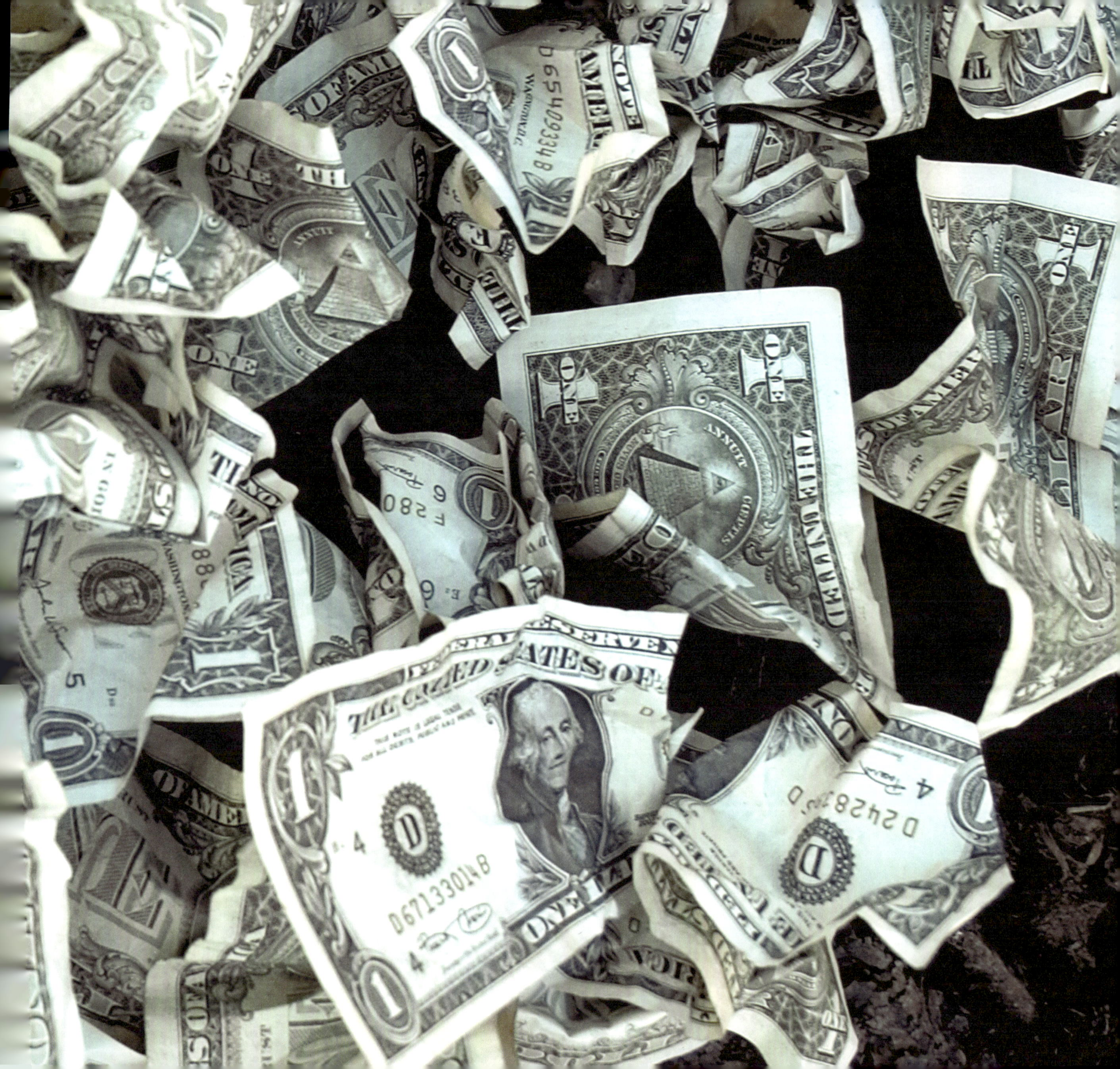